Brimming with God

Brimming with God

Reflecting Theologically on Cases in Ministry

Edited by

Barbara J. Blodgett
and **Matthew Floding**

PICKWICK *Publications* · Eugene, Oregon

Pickwick Publications
An Imprint of Wipf and Stock Publishers
199 W. 8th Ave., Suite 3
Eugene, OR 97401

www.wipfandstock.com

ISBN: 978-1-62564-996-6

Cataloging-in-Publication data:

Brimming with God : reflecting theologically on cases in ministry / edited by Barbara J. Blodgett and Matthew Floding.

xviii + 158 p. ; 23 cm.

ISBN: 978-1-62564-996-6

1. Theology—Study and teaching. I. Blodgett, Barbara J. II. Floding, Matthew. III. Title.

BV4012 W51 2015

Manufactured in the U.S.A.   08/04/2015

In memory of Duane and Ardelle Floding who provided me
with my first formative theological reflections
—MF

In honor of all my students who have taught me
how to do theological reflection
—BJB

Contents

Acknowledgments

MOST BOOKS ARE THE product of some form of collaboration, but this one has been truly collaborative. What began as an idea considered over lunch at a conference eventually turned into a project involving many different people to whom we owe a debt of gratitude. We would like to thank Christine Woodward who formatted the manuscript for us in a timely and efficient manner. We owe gratitude to Herbert Anderson, former editor of *Reflective Practice*, whose encouragement helped us to write and think clearly about methods of theological reflection. We are of course grateful and indebted to all those who contributed to this book—the students who wrote cases for it and our field education colleagues who wrote the reflections. They entrusted us with their experiences, ideas, and words and we hope we have done them justice.

The generous and collegial spirit of the Association for Theological Field Education (ATFE) made possible the level of collaboration necessary to produce this book. Thank you to all of our ATFE colleagues.

Finally, we would like to thank each other. Barbara knows no one who better understands the alchemy of conversation, food, and writing than Matt. His commitment to creating communities of practice sustains her through the more solitary aspects of the writing task. Matt understands that the opportunity to collaborate with Barbara is an opportunity to work with a scholar who is passionately devoted to formational theological education, a colleague who approaches theological reflection with creative flare and a friend who empowers everyone who works with her to push towards excellence.

Contributors

Nannette Banks is the Director of Alumni/ae and Church Relations at McCormick Theological Seminary. She formerly served as the Associate Director of Experiential Education and Field Studies at McCormick and is a past member of the Association for Theological Field Education steering committee. She has engaged in ministry and learning across a myriad of contexts around the world including South Korea, Turkey, Jerusalem, Cairo, London, and Barranquilla. Banks received an MDiv from McCormick Theological Seminary and a Masters in Urban Planning and Policy from the University of Illinois at Chicago.

Barbara J. Blodgett is Assistant Professor of pastoral leadership at Lexington Theological Seminary. She is a minister, educator, and ethicist. She served as Director of Supervised Ministries at Yale Divinity School from 1998–2009. An ordained minister in the United Church of Christ, she has served in parish ministry as well as the national setting of the UCC in addition to field education. She has published three books: *Constructing the Erotic: Sexual Ethics and Adolescent Girls*, *Lives Entrusted: An Ethic of Trust for Ministry*, and *Becoming the Pastor You Hope to Be: Four Practices for Improving Ministry*. Blodgett received an MDiv from Yale Divinity School and a PhD from Yale University.

Annette Brownlee is the Chaplain of Wycliffe College, Director of Field Education, and teaches in the Pastoral Theology Department. Her research interests include the multiple implications of preaching Scripture as the church's book, Augustine's divine pedagogy as a rule of life for preachers, the sermons of André Trocmé, and a model of theological reflection based on the Spirit's use of Scripture in the church. Ordained in the Episcopal Church, she had been in parish ministry in churches in the U.S. for twenty years. She currently assists and preaches at St. Paul's L' Amoreaux, a multi-ethnic immigrant parish in Toronto. Brownlee holds an MDiv from General Theology Seminary in New York and a DMin from Wycliffe College.

Joseph Bush is Director of the Practice of Ministry in Mission at Wesley Theological Seminary. He served as a United Methodist pastor in New Jersey before moving to the Republic of Fiji to teach courses in Ministry at the ecumenical Pacific Theological College. From there, he moved to Dunedin, New Zealand to join a team of colleagues developing a new program in Ordination Studies for the Presbyterian School of Ministry. Most recently prior to Wesley, he was teaching at United Theological Seminary of the Twin Cities in the area of Life and Leadership of the Congregation. His book on pastoral ethics, *Gentle Shepherding*, was named one of the top ten books for 2006 by the Academy of Parish Clergy. Bush earned his MDiv from Wesley Theological Seminary and his PhD from Drew University.

Kimberly Clayton is Director of Contextual Education at Columbia Theological Seminary. She is an ordained minister in the PCUSA and was the Senior Pastor at Grace Covenant Presbyterian Church in Asheville, North Carolina. She also served as Associate Pastor at Central Presbyterian in Atlanta and Hopewell Presbyterian Church in New Jersey. In service to the larger church, she has taught in the Commissioned Lay Pastors training program. Clayton has edited and written several denominational publications including *Members Together: A Guide for New Members*; *Peacemaking in Nehemiah*; and *Older Adult Ministry: A Guide for Sessions and Congregations*. She has also been a contributor to the *Journal for Preachers* and to several volumes of *Feasting on the Word*. Clayton earned her MDiv and DMin at Columbia Theological Seminary.

Emily Click is assistant Dean for Ministry Studies and Field Education and Lecturer on Ministry at Harvard Divinity School. She is ordained in the United Church of Christ and has a decade of congregational ministry experience. She has served as chair of the steering committee of the Association for Theological Field Education. Click teaches courses on leadership and administration, mentoring, and religious education. Publications include "Practical Theology in Contextual Education," in the *Blackwell Companion to Practical Theology*; "Ministerial Reflection," in *Welcome to Theological Field Education*; and "The Evolution of Theological Field Education," in

Equipping the Saints: Best Practices in Contextual Theological Education.
Emily Click earned her MDiv at Bethany Theological Seminary and her
PhD at Claremont School of Theology.

Richard (Dick) Cunningham is Professor Emeritus of Contextual Education for the School of Theology and Ministry at Seattle University. He was
one of the founding members of the School which brings together thir-
teen Protestant traditions and the Roman Catholics under one dean. He
was a member of the core faculty and director of contextual education for
nineteen years. Presently he teaches part time in the new DMin program.
Ordained in the Christian Church (Disciples of Christ), he has been a local
church pastor focusing on youth ministry, the church's educational ministry and social justice. Early in his career he was the DOC's Director of
Youth Ministry for the United States and Canada. He received a DMin degree from Drew University Theological School and an MDiv and an MRel
from Pacific School of Religion.

Deborah Kerr Davis is the Director of field education for Princeton Theological Seminary. She has been the chaplain at the University Medical Center at Princeton and Director of the Department of Religious Ministries for
Princeton HealthCare Systems. She is a member of the Princeton Clergy
Association, and has served as pastor to pastors in New Brunswick Presbytery. She is also trained in spiritual direction. Her MDiv degree is from
Princeton Theological Seminary.

Isabel Docampo is Professor of Supervised Ministry at Perkins School
of Theology. An ordained Baptist minister, she has worked with Latino/a,
Vietnamese, Hmong, and Middle Eastern immigrants. In 2002 she led a
consultation of United Methodist field educators to the Seminario Evan-
gelico de Teologia in Matanzas, Cuba. She co-founded what is now the
Muslim, Jewish and Christian Women's Dialogue Group of Dallas. Docampo's publications include *Joshua, Judges and Ruth* for the New Immersion
Bible Study Series, and several articles and book reviews for the journals
Reflective Practice and the *Journal of Religious Leadership*. Docampo earned
her MDiv from The Southern Baptist Theological Seminary and her DMin
from Perkins.

Matthew Floding is Director of Ministerial Formation and Field Education at Duke Divinity School. An ordained minister in the Reformed Church in America, he has served as pastor, college chaplain and Director of Field Education at Western Theological Seminary in Holland, Michigan. Floding is a past chair of the Steering Committee of The Association for Theological Field Education. He has developed Friendship House, a residential opportunity in which seminarians live in community with persons with intellectual and developmental disabilities, at Western and also at Duke. He is the general editor and contributor to *Welcome to Theological Field Education!* Floding received the MDiv from McCormick Theological Seminary and the DMin from Western Theological Seminary.

Tom Fuller is Director of Ministry Leadership Development, Placement, and Assessment at Beeson Divinity School of Samford University. He teaches courses in ministry leadership and directs the school's programs for theological field education, ministry placement, and assessment of institutional effectiveness. His research interests include student engagement in graduate theological education, assessment of student learning in theological education, and the role of theological field education in ministerial formation. Previously, he served for twelve years as pastor of American Baptist and Southern Baptist churches in Alabama and Indiana. He contributed the chapter "Assessment and Evaluation in Field Education" to *Preparing For Ministry: A Practical Guide to Field Education*. His MDiv and DMin are from The Southern Baptist Theological Seminary and he earned the PhD from the University of Alabama.

Tracy Hartman teaches preaching and directs Supervised Ministry and Doctor of Ministry programs at the Baptist Seminary at Richmond. She is the author of *Letting the Other Speak: Proclaiming the Stories of Biblical Women* and co-author of *New Proclamation Commentary*. She also contributed to the *Feasting on the Word* and *Feasting on the Gospels* commentary series. She served as preacher and lecturer for the First Annual Lay Women's Conference at Baptist Theological Seminary at Zimbabwe. Hartman is active in Baptist life and has served as staff member and interim pastor to several Virginia churches. She enjoys preaching throughout the region. She earned her MDiv degree at Baptist Theological Seminary at Richmond and her PhD at Union Theological Seminary and Presbyterian School of Christian Education.

George Hillman is Chair and Professor of Educational Ministries and Leadership at Dallas Theological Seminary. Prior to joining the seminary faculty, he had several years of ministry experience in churches and parachurch organizations in Texas and Georgia. He is editor of *Preparing for Ministry: A Practical Guide to Theological Field Education* and author of *Ministry Greenhouse: Cultivating Environments for Practical Learning*. He is a former member of the ATFE steering committee and former co-chair of EATFE. He received his MDiv and his PhD from Southwestern Baptist Seminary.

Tara Hornbacker is the Professor of Ministry Formation, Missional Leadership and Evangelism at Bethany Theological Seminary in Richmond, Indiana. She is a coordinator for the Association for the Arts in the Church of the Brethren and serves on the Ministry Advisory Council for the Church of the Brethren Annual Conference. Hornbacker is an ordained minister in the Church of the Brethren and served in pastoral ministry with Church of the Brethren and PCUSA. She holds an MDiv from the Earlham School of Religion and a DMin from Fuller Theological Seminary.

William Kincaid holds the Herald B. Monroe Chair in Practical Parish Ministry and serves as Director of Field Education at Christian Theological Seminary. Kincaid previously served for eleven years as the Senior Minister of Woodland Christian Church (DOC) in Lexington, Kentucky. He was a founding member and later President of The Interfaith Alliance of the Bluegrass. He has also worked as part of the regional ministry team of the Christian Church (DOC) in Kentucky with responsibility for candidates seeking ordination, commissioned, or licensed ministry. Kincaid is the author of two sermon collections and *Finding Voice: How Theological Field Education Shapes Pastoral Identity*. He received his MDiv and DMin from Lexington Theological Seminary and a MS in Higher Education from the University of Kentucky.

Carol Kuzmochka is a part-time professor at Saint Paul University, Ottawa, where she teaches practical theology, pastoral practice, professional ministry practicum, and religious education. A Roman Catholic, she has been the Director of the Centre for Ministry Formation at Saint Paul University, a formation consultant and adviser to The Oblates of Mary Immaculate

(Lacombe Province, Canada), the Director of Adult Faith Formation for the Archdiocese of Ottawa and the Diocese of Timmins, and a Consultant and Process Facilitator for numerous parishes and religious organizations. Kuzmochka's DMin degree/Doctorat en théologie practique is from Saint Paul University, Ottawa.

Viki Matson is the Director of Field Education and Assistant Professor of the Practice of Ministry at Vanderbilt Divinity School. Prior to Vanderbilt, she served as Chaplain at St. Thomas Hospital in Nashville, Tennessee. Matson holds an MDiv from Phillips Theological Seminary. Additionally, she has completed a residency year in Clinical Pastoral Education and has done graduate study in Ethics. She is ordained in the Christian Church (DOC). Matson has served on the steering committee of the Association for Theological Field Education.

Kathleen Sams Russell is the Joe and Jesse Crump Associate Professor of Cultural Research and Associate Professor of Pastoral Theology at Seminary of the Southwest where she also directs the theological field education program. Prior to joining the seminary faculty, she served as a pediatric chaplain at Children's National Medical Center in Washington, DC, supervised CPE students in San Diego and Washington, DC, and did community organizing in South Carolina and Chicago. Ordained in the Episcopal Church, Russell has also been involved in parish ministry. Her areas of expertise include theological reflection for ministry formation, pastoral care, and vocational development in the context of human growth and personality. Russell received her MDiv from Seabury-Western Theological Seminary and a DMin from Austin Presbyterian Theological Seminary.

Christian Batalden Scharen is Vice President for Applied Research and Co-Director of the Center for the Study of Theological Education at Auburn Theological Seminary. He previously was Director of Contextual Education and Assistant Professor of Worship and Theology at Luther Seminary, directed the Faith as a Way of Life Project at Yale Divinity School, and led the Congregational Responses to Community Crisis Project at Candler School of Theology. His publications include *Perspectives in Ecclesiology and Ethnography, Broken Hallelujahs: Why Popular Music Matters to Those Seeking God,* and *Ethnography as Christian Theology and Ethics.* Scharen's PhD is from Emory University and he is an ordained pastor in the Evangelical Lutheran Church in America.

Lorraine Ste-Marie is Associate Professor, Faculty of Human Sciences and Director of the Master of Pastoral Theology and Doctor of Ministry Programs at Saint Paul University in Ottawa. She is the past Chair of the Association of Theological Field Education. A Roman Catholic, she received her MA (Theology, Ethics Concentration) at Saint Paul University and her DMin at McMaster University. She is the author of *Beyond Words: New Language for a Changing Church* and contributed the chapter "Language and Leadership" to *Welcome to Theological Field Education.*

Sue Withers is is presently the Field Education Co-ordinator within the Uniting Church Theological College in Australia. She is an ordained Uniting Church minister who has served in various ministries across the Uniting Church. She worked for twenty years in school chaplaincy and education and was a Presbytery Minister and Moderator within the Synod of Victoria and Tasmania. Withers is presently completing a Grad. Dip. in Psychology at Monash University and regularly leads worship at a local Uniting Church in Hampton.

Roslyn Wright is Director of Field Education at Whitley College, a college of the University of Divinity, Melbourne. Ordained by the Baptist Union of Victoria, Australia, she has served as both an associate and a senior pastor. Prior to pastoral ministry, Roslyn worked in primary (elementary) school education, adult employment training, and industrial chaplaincy. She is president of the Australian and New Zealand Association for Theological Field Education (ANZATFE). Wright earned both her MA in Spiritual Direction and her MTS from Melbourne College of Divinity.

Christina Zaker is the Director of Field Education at Catholic Theological Union. A Roman Catholic, she has worked in a variety of ministerial settings including parish ministry, retreat work, campus ministry, and as the executive director of Amate House, the young adult volunteer program for the Archdiocese of Chicago. Zaker's work has appeared in *US Catholic Magazine*, the *National Catholic Reporter* and *Reflective Practice: Formation and Supervision in Ministry*. She received her DMin, with a focus on theological reflection, from Catholic Theological Union.

Student Case Contributors

Cathy Caldwell Hoop
Tracy Huselton
Anne Katherine Ritchey
Nash Smith
David Wantland

1

Introduction

Barbara Blodgett and Matthew Floding

THEOLOGICAL FIELD EDUCATION PROVIDES places to practice ministry and spaces to reflect theologically on that experience to the end that the student experiences growth toward ministerial competency that has theological integrity. *Welcome to Theological Field Education*, written by theological field educators, in large part addressed place and process in field education.[1] The question of how theological reflection is integrated into and practiced within field education is explored in this book, also written by field educators.

Theological reflection is a cornerstone of all field education programs, where it is a pedagogical practice leveraging the experiences of students in order to form them as ministers. Formation in ministry has to do with developing competencies, to be sure, but it also has to do with meaning-making. Students in field education learn to minister authentically and faithfully by learning to make sense of themselves and their experiences. This work takes space and time and a community of practice that invites accountability. The practice of theological reflection, however it is done, creates the space for communal meaning-making that forms thoughtful and competent ministers who minister with integrity and faithfulness.

Of course, field educators are not alone among those who are interested in the search for meaning and faithfulness in the practice of ministry, or in religious experience more generally. Practical theologians have for

---

1. Floding, *Welcome to Theological Field Education*.

years addressed questions of experience and meaning-making. How do individuals, groups, and congregations bring the Christian tradition to bear upon their experiences as Christians, so as to understand them theologically? This might be the central question of theological reflection; the question of how to put tradition and experience into genuine conversation with each other has no easy answer.

A simple way to visualize theological reflection might be as a Venn diagram—the intersection between two circles forming a space of meaning created when experience, on the one hand, is brought together with tradition, on the other.[2] The conversation "opens the gates between our experience and our Christian heritage," wrote Patricia O'Connell Killen and John de Beer, the theologian and educator who have arguably had the greatest influence over field educators' practice of theological reflection.[3] But when the gates are opened, it is all too easy for the conversation to slide in one direction or the other. As reflectors, we may fall back too quickly on tradition as the definitive interpreter of experience and miss the new meanings being made. Alternatively, we might selectively hand pick from tradition those insights that merely confirm what we have already decided is meaningful about our experience.[4] What we desire is a genuine, mutually informing and influencing dialogue between the two that produces new meaning(s).

Among theologians, a model called the "revised correlational model" rose to prominence as an answer to that desire. Inspired by the work of David Tracy, theologians correlate elements of theological tradition with concrete situations in human life. As Don Browning defined the model: "In general terms, a revised correlational program in theology attempts to correlate critically both the questions and answers about human existence derived from an interpretation of the central Christian witness *with* the questions and answers implicit in various interpretations of ordinary human experience."[5] Or as Lewis Mudge and James Poling put it even more succinctly: "*Some* interpretation of the tradition comes together with *some* interpretation of the situation to create a possibly unprecedented

2. Killen and de Beer, *The Art of Theological Reflection*, ix.

3. Ibid., viii.

4. Killen and de Beer call these two fallback positions, respectively, "the standpoint of certitude" and "the standpoint of self-assurance." Ibid., 4–13.

5. See Don Browning, "Practical Theology and Religious Education," in Mudge and Poling, *Formation and Reflection*, 80; italics in original. See also Tracy, *Blessed Rage*.

articulation of the faith."[6] The "possibly unprecedented articulation of the faith" could be a way of describing that space of intersection in a Venn diagram.

What field educators may be said to contribute to this broad theological project is a certain very practical concern: field educators, as we said above, seek to form individuals into ministers. Generally speaking, our aim is not to articulate the Christian faith in unprecedented ways. We leave that constructive task to systematic and practical theologians. Nevertheless, our own task is a challenging and sophisticated one. Formation is a hugely complex process. Education for ministry is simultaneously intellectual, practical, and spiritual. Not only must ministry students today develop and hone endless competencies for future ministry, but they are expected to integrate competencies as diverse as biblical exegesis, ethical reasoning, and listening skills for intercultural communication. Their contexts for practicing ministry vary tremendously. Future cathedral deans prepare for ministry alongside founders of house churches; non-profit CEOs alongside college chaplains. The communities in which they will eventually minister make conflicting and at times even contradictory demands of their preparation. Theological and pedagogical approaches to theological education have proliferated in recent years. Even the definition of 'ministry' is contested. All this is to say that if theological reflection is in itself challenging, theological reflection done in the service of ministerial formation is even more so. "Reflect theologically on an experience you have had in your internship" is far easier said than done.

It should come as no surprise, then, that when as editors we launched this book project, we ourselves underestimated the challenge of asking a group of field educators from across the spectrum of theological education to write theological reflections on cases in ministry. Several times we found ourselves redefining the invitation, so diverse in style and approach were the responses we received. And yet we feel the end result gives an accurate portrayal both of the diversity of what this group means by 'theological reflection' and the commitment we share to forming reflective practitioners.

Nearly three decades ago a group of practical theologians, including both theorists and practitioners, were gathered in an attempt to close the gap between academic theology and the life of faith—"tradition and situation," as they called it. Many of the essays that resulted discussed the revised correlation method. The group's conveners, Lewis Mudge and James Poling,

---

6. Mudge and Poling, *Formation and Reflection,* xxiv; italics in original.

acknowledged that methods of theological reflection seemed to proliferate even more wildly when the rubber hits the road in practice, so to speak:

> What will happen if these different ways of reflecting on the encounter of tradition with situation are deliberately brought down into the lassitude, the confusion, the passion (whatever the case may be) of the formation process among actual human beings and tested there for cogency? The practitioners among our contributors . . . have done this systematically, but the theorists have not. Will there be an uncovering of a 'generative grammar' of formation underlying all the manifest differences? Will the different conceptualizations used in such reflection-in-formation prove, in this process, to be tolerable translations of each other? Or will they themselves look like a new field of irreducible pluralism?[7]

We recognize in Mudge's and Poling's questions inquiries that lie at the heart of *Brimming with God*. Theological field education is currently brimming with different ways of doing theological reflection on the ground. Our collaborators in *this* book do not all employ the same grammar when describing what they do with students, or why. Approaches to theological reflection have proliferated. And yet, we believe that they are not irreducibly pluralistic. This project tests that hunch.

THEOLOGICAL REFLECTION DEFINED

We offered the following basic conceptualization of theological reflection to our collaborators when we invited them into this project, and we offer it here as well for our readers. It is risky to attempt any single definition. But let us risk generalization and define theological reflection in field education as *reflection upon lived, embodied experiences in ministry that seeks to make sense of practice and form reflectors in habits for competent ministry.* We shall expand on each part of this definition in turn.

Experience

Field educators keep theological reflection inescapably grounded in experience. Reasons for doing so are both pedagogical and philosophical. Pedagogically speaking, the heart of most field education programs is the time

7. Ibid., xxvi.

students spend actually practicing ministry in the field. The accumulated and assorted experiences from that practice become the 'assigned text' within this area of the theological curriculum. Field education students may spend time reading and writing, but reading and writing are not the central activities of field education. Field education is premised on the conviction that one learns by reflecting on doing—indeed, that one *can* learn by reflecting *solely* on doing—and consequently, the doing of ministry is its ultimate ground. Indeed, though students who identify as their primary learning goal the simple 'Gain experience in ministry' may make field educators wish for loftier aims, those students are not (in one sense) far off the mark. They recognize that nothing substitutes for experience as a source of learning and reflection, and if they bring little experience to bear upon the enterprise of ministerial reflection, they will learn no more than students of classical theology who never crack open their texts. In field education, for better or worse, experience is the raw material—or primary text, if you will—that we have to work with in formation. Admittedly this material gets filtered through an interpretive lens before it even reaches the supervisory conversation or peer reflection group, but if there is anything distinctive about the pedagogy of field education within theological education curriculum, it is this.

More philosophically, field educators would generally situate themselves on the 'experience' side of the Venn diagram. In other words, they tend to start the process of theological reflection there. Another way of putting it is to reference a continuum created by James Whitehead and Evelyn Eaton Whitehead. They argued that reflections on faith occur along a continuum from 'Ministry' to 'Theology.' Reflections differ according to whether they "are more influenced by the immediacy of a pastoral concern or by the historical, scriptural, or philosophical complexity of a religious question."[8] Reflections that are immediate and concrete in their concern, are produced in one or two sessions, and take personal and ministerial experience as conversation partners, characterize the 'ministry' end. On the 'theology' end, reflections are broad in scope, ongoing and extended in time, and recognize philosophy and history as conversation partners. An intermediate position views theological reflection as concerned with pastoral situations in context, done over several weeks or months, and drawing upon theology as well as social sciences.[9] We would argue that most field educators would

8. Whitehead and Whitehead, *Method in Ministry*, xi.

9. See Figure 1 in ibid., xii.

locate their theological reflection practice somewhere between the 'intermediate' and 'ministry' points on the Whiteheads' continuum.

What the privileging of experience means from the perspective of this book is that many (though not all) of our collaborators take the details of the case they are reflecting on as their starting point, and develop as careful and accurate a picture of what is going on as possible before turning to the resources of Christian tradition. As a result, the turn to tradition may at times look like a "scrolling through" Bible, theology, ethics, pastoral theology, and so on, to see what might apply to the case. But again, field educators are not as concerned to construct new theological meaning as they are to begin making sense of a complex experience laid before them.

Lived

As Mudge and Poling recognized, theological reflection in formation can and must take the messiness of context into account. In their ministry practice every week, students encounter sin as well as redemption, judgment alongside love, finitude counterbalanced by freedom. Many different scriptural passages speak to them. Many moments from their own past experience come to mind, as well as wisdom from the Christian tradition. Their ministry practice prompts them to recall knowledge and skills from the social sciences and other disciplines. We are using the term 'lived' to suggest that conscious interpretation begins with situations as they are actually made manifest, whether or not they neatly correspond to inherited theological categories, scriptural texts, or other lessons. On one level, of course, all experience is necessarily lived (what would 'unlived' experience be, after all?), but what we emphasize in our use of this modifier is the desire within theological reflection to let the contradictions and inconsistencies stand, for as long as possible. Reflection upon experience, like any way of "seeing anew," can all too quickly produce a 20/20 image without acknowledging the refraction. Our collaborators consistently resist premature correlations, and often express their ideas in the form of questions. In so doing, they are allowing for the possibility that if the case's context were to shift, or time were to pass, their theological reflection might be quite different.

Embodied

By "embodied," we mean that the practice of ministry is experienced with the whole self—intellectual, affective, spiritual, and physical—and so, too, is reflection upon it. Naming these dimensions and incorporating them into theological reflection lends integrity to its practice. Patricia O'Connell Killen writes that "reflection begins when one pauses and ponders" about an incident and is best done when one does not try to "wrest meaning from [the] incident."[10] She is writing about the reflection that teachers do on their practices of teaching, but her insights pertain equally well to students of ministry starting theological reflection. In a nod to the embodied nature of reflection, Killen stresses the importance of retaining the "affective connection" to events being reflected upon. She is convinced that it is the combination of affective connection and intellectual distance that causes reflection to work. Although seemingly contradictory impulses, affective connection and intellectual distance together produce meaning. While intellectual distance allows reflectors to step back and gain the kind of perspective that comes from thinking a little more theoretically, affective connection allows them to stay close to the event and to keep its experience fresh by continuing to feel it.

In this book, nearly all of our collaborators explore the affective dimensions of their case, primarily by interpreting the emotions and feelings of the characters in it, but also at times by naming their own affective connection to it. In addition, at least one collaborator attempts to 'see,' 'hear,' and 'feel' the case's context as if he were walking through it, thus approximating a more literally embodied mode of reflection that some field educators prefer to employ whenever they are able (through field trips, immersion experiences, and the like).

To Make Sense of Practice

As articulated above, ministerial practice has to do with both meaning and competency. Field education aims at both. Field educators seek to form students of ministry who are both competent at their practice and able to make sense of it.[11] Often in their eagerness to become successful at minis-

---

10. Killen, "Midrange Reflection," 144.

11. Keeping both goals in mind is the reason that many field educators, including Emily Click, have begun referring to theological reflection as ministerial reflection. For

try, students tend to privilege the former. They want to know what to do and how to do it, whether the task is worship leadership, pastoral care, or growing their church. They may initially be quite uninterested in what these tasks *mean* and how to re-envision them for ministry today. But field educators try to follow the rhythm of first asking, 'What does this mean?' and only later asking, 'What should we do?'

Ironically, then, one of the best starting points for theological reflection is an event whose meaning is unclear! While the overall aim may be making sense of ministry practice, reflection is often effectively triggered by something discordant that does not make immediate sense or for which multiple interpretations are possible. After all, as our field education colleague Abigail Johnson points out, humans engage in reflection all the time—even through the act of dreaming—in order to make sense of their daily lives. Reflection becomes more deliberate as life events become more "unsettling": "Most of the time, our reflection is unconscious, helping us to put our world in order . . . Yet not all our reflection is unconscious. At times we need to deal with situations and issues that demand attention. Usually what stands out is an event that touches our feelings or unsettles our ways of thinking."[12]

A student might experience a ministry event that doesn't make sense because it is unusual or unexpected, but events worth reflecting on do not necessarily have to be negative. The salient feature of a theological reflection event is its disruptive quality. As Killen writes: "Humans tend to pay attention to events, interactions, or texts when they disrupt habitual processes and categories of interpretation. Exquisite beauty, moral collapse, personal loss, intense conflict, a gap between aspiration and fulfillment, and more may grasp our attention."[13] Disruptive events grasp students' attention and become fodder for reflection because they are literally nonsensical, at least for a time, and demand that sense be made of them. In keeping with the conviction that theological reflection is best when it stems from a desire for coherence or clarity, every case in this book began its life as an event that grasped the author's attention.

Disruptive does not necessarily mean sensational. Even ordinary events are disruptive, and therefore provide interest, when examined

a helpful description of the practice see Emily Click, "Ministerial Reflection," in Floding, *Welcome to Theological Field Education*, 31–43.

12. Johnson, *Reflecting With God*, 25.

13. Killen, "Midrange Reflection," 144.

closely enough. Sometimes the best theological reflection is generated by seemingly trivial events that at first glance seem idiosyncratic to one student's ministry but yield layers of meaning and eventually become relevant to everyone. So long as they somehow disrupt traditional categories of interpretation and cause reflectors to take a second look at what happened to them, simple events matter in theological reflection.

In this book, we seek to demonstrate this last point by presenting cases that reflect ordinary stories in the lives of ordinary practitioners of ministry. While we strove to achieve a diverse array of cases in terms of denominational context, geographical setting, and area of ministerial skill, we also wanted cases that would be widely recognizable. Some cases were written by our collaborators' students and some were written by and about our collaborators themselves. They are admittedly skewed toward challenges and disappointments in ministry, because as one of our collaborators points out, case writers tend to gravitate toward events that have *not* gone particularly well. But unlike the kinds of cases used in some other realms of professional education (medicine, engineering), we have not selected cases that break new ground by virtue of their unusual or novel content.

Finally, with respect to making sense of ministry practice, field education tends to encourage multiple meanings to emerge. In other words, our theological reflection tends to eschew 'right answers.' It ultimately favors what theologians call 'thick descriptions' over quick answers. As Herbert Anderson says, "insisting on 'thick descriptions' is a way of ensuring that we hear the whole story, listen for unheard voices, leave no stone unturned" in our reflection.[14] At the point of meaning-making, many field educators insist that there be no single theological or ministerial meaning assigned to a particular experience. Rather, students are invited to bring their diverse and distinctive perspectives to bear upon the same event, often resulting in more than one interpretation. Not all theological interpretations are affirmed as equally valid.[15] But theological reflection in formation is especially open to multi-layered, richly textured ways of sense-making.

Readers may at times feel as though a few stones *should* have been left unturned, so comprehensive are some of the analyses in this book. Many of our collaborators were attempting to demonstrate in one brief essay the

14. Herbert Anderson, personal communication.

15. See Herbert Anderson's interaction with Amy Plantinga Pauw and Randy Maddox on integrity in "Authenticity and Character in Pastoral Ministry," in Cameron et al., *Together in Ministry*, 161–62.

richness of a classroom conversation with their students that would have unfolded over an hour or more. Readers may also sense that some cases remain unresolved even after reflection. If so, they are sensing what students sense in an actual theological reflection discussion! We invite readers to imagine what *they* might have said or written about each case, rendering the 'thick description' even thicker.

To Form Reflectors in Habits for Competent Ministry

Field educators often like to reserve the question of 'What should we do?' until students have sufficiently pondered the meaning of their experience. The 'point' of theological reflection is not to arrive at the correct steps a student should take next in his or her internship. But theological reflection *is* ultimately a practical enterprise, and its fruits are borne out in students' further practice of ministry. Theological reflection shapes students' thinking in all the ways described above: by slowing down the interpretive process, letting the affective dimensions of experience become informative, and resisting premature conclusions. But it also shapes the way students do ministry by forming them in habits, some of which will be more fitting than others. In sifting through the multiple ways to view a given event in ministry, more or less authentic ways of acting as a minister emerge. Simply put, some actions more appropriately follow reflection than others. As a result of doing theological reflection over time, habits of responding in fitting manners are developed and become second-nature; a student of ministry is aided thereby in practicing ministry authentically.

Ultimately, theological reflection shapes students' sense of identity, their very being. Pastoral imagination becomes stretched and invigorated by the discipline of engaging in it regularly. Practicing it over time enables students to listen more attentively to meanings in their own and others' lives. They learn in their reflection groups how to live reflective lives more generally. As Craig Dykstra notes, "What we see depends not only what is in front of our eyes, but also on what lies within our hearts and minds."[16] Or as one of our collaborators put it, "theological reflection becomes an ongoing habit, an orientation to the world, a way of thinking and being that infuses all they do."[17] By continually seeing how actions in ministry reflect and embody the values of Scripture, tradition, and experience, they learn

16. Dykstra, *Vision and Character*, 50.

17. Viki Matson, personal communication.

to align their own habits and actions with their deepest values. Ultimately theological reflection becomes a spiritual practice as well as an intellectual one that students of ministry will carry with them throughout their ministry careers.

Having sketched a basic definition of theological reflection that we feel serves more or less well all of the reflections in this book, let us now examine some of the similarities and differences among the ways our collaborators approached the task.

CONCEPTUALIZATIONS OF THEOLOGICAL REFLECTION

Field educators describe what they do when they do theological reflection in many different ways. Some of their descriptions reflect, either consciously or not, the basic idea of a many-sided conversation where some kind of correlation is going on. Kincaid (who acknowledges his indebtedness to Don Browning and the concept of mutual critical correlation) describes the task as "getting different boxes to talk to each other." Fuller correlates Scripture with experience but assigns to Scripture the role of "normative backstop." He implies that there are bounds to the normative conclusions one might draw about a case, and Scripture provides them. Several others rely on the Whiteheads' idea of a triangle (or other shape), that is, theological reflection is a matter of bringing several 'points' together, especially the three points of human experience as described in the case, cultural and sociological factors in the case, and religious tradition.[18] Click describes reflection as a process of correlating "conflicting interplay between layers" that starts with identifying feelings but includes deeper interpersonal and organizational dynamics at play in a case and even its possible legal ramifications. While none of our collaborators explicitly name the Wesleyan Quadrilateral as their methodology, many of their reflections suggest an equally-weighted reliance on Scripture, tradition, reason, and experience as conversation partners.

Some of our collaborators liken the process of theological reflection to the movement around a circle or spiral. Harkening to social theorists and experiential learning theorists as well as many theologians, they trace a basic action-reflection-action loop in their reflections. Theological reflection has a trajectory; it is a matter of "working through" reactions on the way to something else, and it is a "continual process."

18. Whitehead and Whitehead, *Method in Ministry*, 6.

With a play on the literal meaning of reflection, many describe the theological reflection task in visual terms—the aim is to "see with new eyes," "acquire vision," "attend," "view reality through a wide-angle lens," "change perception," and "let insight emerge from quagmires." Zaker talks specifically about the new vision coming initially in the form of a "surprise" that yields insight.

Many of our collaborators write about theological reflection as inquiry and exploration. Question-posing dominates their methods. Theological reflection "opens a space for exploration," creates a "pathway in" to experience and ultimately forms students as good inquirers themselves. Some emphasize the mystery and open-ended nature of their method, like the way Withers describe her task as "entering a new space not knowing where it will go."

METHODS OF THEOLOGICAL REFLECTION

Given the diversity of approaches our collaborators used when reflecting theologically on their cases, and also acknowledging that the cases themselves often likely dictated which approach they would take, it is risky to categorize the approaches used in this book according to collaborator. Nevertheless, certain groupings do seem to emerge when the reflections are compared with each other. Some collaborators we put in more than one group.

What/So What/Now What

With humor and humility, one of our collaborators suggests that since in practice "sometimes theological reflection can appear to be multifaceted and cumbersome" it might helpfully be boiled down to three simple questions: *What? So What?* and *Now What?* In other words, reflectors first spend time becoming aware of all that is going on in an experience, then they examine what meaning might be made of that experience (through some form of correlation) and finally they propose what could be done next.

The majority of our collaborators chose some method that could be described this way. They do not always follow precisely three steps, and they give their steps a variety of interesting and creative names, but their reflections share a basic common formula of moving from the present case to its meaning and on toward future possibilities. In this category we would include:

- Nannette Banks (Insertion, Social Analysis, Theological Reflection, Pastoral Planning)
- Emily Click (Feelings, Images, Theological Issues, Future Ministerial Action)
- Kimberly Clayton (Entering the Experience and Identifying the Heart of the Matter, Searching for Insight and Broadening the Conversation, Action Moving Forward)
- Richard Cunningham (What? So What? Now What?)
- **Matthew Floding (What do I see? and Why did this happen? How does scripture speak? and What is at stake theologically? How might we respond?)**
- Tom Fuller (Observations, Engagement, Response)
- Tracy Hartman (Cultural Issues, Personal Experience, Scripture and Tradition, Future Praxis)
- George Hillman (Christian Scripture, Christian Heritage, Cultural Experience, Personal Experience, Application)
- Tara Hornbacker (What is Really Going On Here? Where is God in All This? What is Mine to Do?)
- William Kincaid (Minister and Experience, Gospel and Context, Toward a Faithful Response)
- Lorraine Ste-Marie and Carol Kuzmochka (Attending, Asserting, Deciding)
- Roslyn Wright (Action, Reaction, Reflection, Response)
- Christina Zaker (Recognizing the Familiar, Seeking the Surprise, Acknowledging the Invitation).

Neo-liberal Theology and Ministry

Annette Brownlee's approach may on the surface appear to belong in the category above, but her insistence that reflection be done in light of a prior theological understanding of ministry makes her approach sufficiently distinct, in our view. It reminds us of the way a camera zooms out and then back in: she moves from describing what is going on in the case, to Scripture, then beyond Scripture to God's actions through Christ's ministry as known in Scripture, then back to reflectors' participation in Christ's ministry, and finally back to the case.

Theology and Practice

While Viki Matson's approach does aim toward future practice, and she identifies her approach with an action-reflection-action circle, her starting point is unapologetically one of theological questions. For her, theology informs practice and practice then expresses theological claims. Chris Scharen's method is one of attending to and listening to the other with all one's senses. In his method, theology and practice cannot easily be separated.

Transcendental

Sue Withers employs a transcendental method of theological reflection that drew her into the case as a subject herself whose own search for self-awareness added meaning to the case.

Social Theory/Analysis

A group of collaborators explicitly analyze cases from a perspective of social and political theory. These would include:

- Nannette Banks (the pastoral circle linking faith with social justice)
- Isabel Docampo (postcolonial liberation theology)
- Tracy Hartman (social psychology on perceptions of race).

Communication Theories

For two of our collaborators, their cases allow them the opportunity to demonstrate theologically-based communication theories:

Joseph Bush (practical hermeneutics for cross-cultural communication)

Deborah Kerr Davis (compassionate communication theory)

Narrative Theories

A cluster of collaborators employ some form of narrative theory, treating cases as stories that could be analyzed as such. Narrative theory in turn might rest upon postmodern deconstruction of narratives.

Barbara Blodgett (narrative therapy)

Kathleen Russell (narrative approach emerging from a theology of incarnation)

Christina Zaker (theological reflection in a parabolic mode)

GRAMMARS OF FORMATION

Ultimately, the methods of theological reflection that field educators choose and practice with students reflect their understandings of formation. Recalling Mudge and Poling's question, is there a "generative grammar" of formation underlying the diversity of approaches to reflection depicted above? Although methods and practices of formation were not the focus of this book, our collaborators nevertheless often drew connections between their approach to theological reflection and their overall goals for their students' formation. How would they define the formation that their practice of theological reflection supports? They describe it as "being fieldworkers in theology," "becoming storytellers," "developing pastoral agility and flexibility," "being able to bring healing and reconciliation to a globalized world of suffering," "becoming imaginative and resilient leaders," "transcending ourselves," "framing the pastoral care of the Church in light of God's care of us," "surfacing the true self," "developing the muscle of curiosity, the heart of engagement, and the ear of listening," "forming wise practitioners," "choosing a generous response," "going deeper into the mystery," "cultivating the good news in our ministry," "developing habits of observation, deep listening, and reflection," "becoming aware that all our work is worship," "learning to heal, redeem, and liberate." We leave it to the reader to decide whether this pluralism represents a sign of concern or a sign of hope for the formation of future ministers, but we see field education brimming with hope.

THE USE OF CASES FOR THEOLOGICAL REFLECTION

Cases have long been a favorite starting point for theological reflection.[19] We use them in this book because we wish to simulate how a group might practice theological reflection. Cases let an experience be reflected upon by a wider circle of reflectors than just the practitioner alone. A case is basically a brief narrative of a ministry event that has recently happened or is currently unfolding. Like a pebble cast into a pond that forms concentric rings on the surface of the water as its impact is felt, a case allows a student to "drop" a piece of her experience into a space for reflection. What starts as her own individual experience and reflection upon experience becomes absorbed by the group, and they make it at least in part their own.[20] Some of the cases in this book are written in the first person, and some in the third person. Most of our contributors chose to reflect on them in the third-person composite voice of a reflection group. Others adopted the first-person voice of the case writer, while at least one wrote as if transcribing a group discussion.

OUTLINE OF THE BOOK

In this book, we paired two collaborators with each other, each writing a reflection on the same case. Therefore, each chapter is formatted in the same way, as follows: First, each collaborator describes her or his method of theological reflection. Frequently they additionally comment on each other's methods. The case follows these introductions. The two reflections follow the case. Each chapter concludes with one or two discussion question that readers might use individually or in their own reflection groups.

---

19. In 1993, a group of field educators wrote a helpful and concise guide to the use of cases in field education. We refer readers to this resource for a more in-depth explanation of the use of cases in theological reflection. See Mahan, Troxell, and Allen, *Shared Wisdom*.

20. We are indebted to Abigail Johnson for this metaphor. She argues that theological reflections' impact is not only made on reflectors themselves and their reflection groups, but also on their congregations. "A stone tossed into a pond sinks to the bottom unseen, yet outward ripples on the surface of the water demonstrate the lingering effect of the stone's impact. The lingering effect of small groups engaging in theological reflection makes an impact on the ongoing life of a congregation." See Johnson, *Reflecting with God*, 91.

BIBLIOGRAPHY

Cameron, Heather et al., eds. *Together in Ministry: Essays to Honour John Paver*. Parkville, Vic: Uniting Academic, 2009.

Dykstra, Craig. *Vision and Character*. Eugene, OR: Wipf & Stock, 2008.

Floding, Matthew, ed. *Welcome to Theological Field Education*. Herndon, VA: The Alban Institute, 2011.

Johnson, Abigail. *Reflecting With God: Connecting Faith and Daily Life in Small Groups*. Herndon, VA: Alban Institute, 2004.

Killen, Patricia O'Connell. "Midrange Reflection: The Underlying Practice of Wabash Center Worships, Colloquies, and Consultations." *Teaching Theology & Religion* 10.3 (2007) 143–49.

Killen, Patricia O'Connell, and John de Beer. *The Art of Theological Reflection*. New York: Crossroad, 1994.

Mahan, Jeffrey H., Barbara B. Troxell, and Carol J. Allen. *Shared Wisdom: A Guide to Case Study Reflection in Ministry*. Nashville: Abingdon, 1993.

Mudge, Lewis S., and James N. Poling, eds. *Formation and Reflection: The Promise of Practical Theology*. Philadelphia: Fortress, 1987.

Tracy, David. *Blessed Rage for Order: The New Pluralism in Theology*. New York: Seabury, 1975.

Whitehead, James D., and Evelyn Eaton Whitehead. *Method in Ministry: Theological Reflection and Christian Ministry*. Rev. ed. Lanham, MD: Sheed & Ward, 1995.

2

Fearfully and Wonderfully Made

Viki Matson and Christian Scharen

INTRODUCTION

Matson:

ONE OF MY PRIMARY goals in theological field education is to help students understand how deeply connected are theology and practice. Any practice of religious leadership (i.e. what we *do*) betrays our theological claims (i.e. what we *think* and *believe*), and our theological claims inform wise pastoral practice. In the way that breathing consists of our conscious or unconscious inhaling and exhaling, so, too, wise religious leadership should be marked by acts of kindness, mercy and justice that have been steeped in intentional theological reflection. It ought to be theologically clear why we do things in the way we do them. Getting this clarity often begins with questions. It's tempting to want to fix the problem, to smooth over conflict, to perhaps even psychoanalyze or offer social analysis. While these can, at times, be important dimensions of religious leadership, it is not at the heart of who we are.

My method of theological reflection, therefore, begins with theological questions. I believe that reflectors start by listening very carefully to contexts, encounters, conversations and dilemmas so that they can discern the spoken and unspoken questions that are present. Then I bring to bear *on those questions* the resources of theology and faith. It is important at this point to name all the things that are sources of our theologizing. That is, from whence do we get our theology? Sources include traditional ones such as Scripture, tradition, community, and family, as well as experience and reason (from the Wesleyan Quadrilateral). Many dimensions of life contribute to the theological construction of our faith claims, including intuitions, oppressions, identities, suffering, and privilege. In particular, experiences with tragedy and disruption often form the occasion for re-thinking theological claims.

The exercise of naming sources demonstrates that there are several possible pathways into engaging in theological reflection upon a situation or a case study. Different reflectors will start in different places. For those who come from a tradition or denomination for whom Scripture is a central authority, they might want to start with the biblical text. Others might prefer to start with a particular theological doctrine, perhaps re-evaluating what they have been taught and thinking their way into a more life-giving option. Still others might want to consider the event through a particular hermeneutical lens. For my purposes here I offer some seeds of theological reflection from each of these starting points that might provide some pathways for thinking about the particular dilemmas raised in this case.

Chris's reflection is a reminder of the deep listening (to words, silences, sighs) that is essential for the work of theological field education. It calls to mind the careful observation work of nature writer Annie Dillard, who studies one plot of ground so closely that she notices the slightest of movements as well as systemic changes over time.[1] This work of paying attention to context, text, persons, and worldviews is fundamental to making theological sense of a dilemma.

My approach, which assumes the careful listening that Chris describes, steers us a bit more conscientiously into that which comprises a theological curriculum. I am eager to integrate theology and practice by bringing both into intentional conversation with each other. Chris's work is an important reminder that the work of integration cannot happen without the primary and ongoing work of tending to what is there and not there.

---

1. Dillard, *Pilgrim*.

Scharen:

I use the phrase 'fieldwork in theology' as a frame for understanding theological field education and more generally the craft of field research for ministry. 'Fieldwork in theology' is a phrase suggesting the student-minister is doing careful listening to a particular context, and doing it both with the conviction that God is at work there, and that one's own listening is holy work, a participation in God's work.

The basic idea comes from sociologist Pierre Bourdieu, who in order to describe his approach to social science once used the phrase 'fieldwork in philosophy.' He meant a couple things by this phrase. First, he was originally trained in philosophy, so the frameworks and modes of thinking he learned in philosophy flow into and influence his sociological fieldwork. Second, he pushes against the idea that one can divide theory and method; instead, he views fieldwork as theoretically freighted.[2] This can easily fit with theology and the research of theological students. They, too, are for the most part first trained in theology and receive some level of introduction to the practice of fieldwork along the way. Further, fieldwork is theologically freighted. Said differently, you don't bring theological concepts to an atheological situation and apply them, as one might apply butter on a piece of toast. Rather, both you and the context are brimming with God, and the question is one of frameworks of attention and understanding.

This is where we need to begin. In order to engage fieldwork in theology, you already have all the tools you need: your body, with its kinetic capacities, its senses, and so on. By paying careful attention, and then trying to find words for what they see and hear, reflectors open themselves to the other, ultimately forgetting themselves and letting the other speak. The use of cases does admittedly reduce the capacities reflectors are able to bring to bear on a situation, since they can't physically walk through the context. Actually being physically present is a much more formative practice. But they can still be led deeply into a context by a good case.

It is fitting that the case itself demonstrates people engaged in an exercise of attending to the other. In this way the situation in the case mirrors my own method of hearing and understanding the other as fully as one is able.

2. Bourdieu, *In Other Words*, 28.

THE CASE

Context

Neighborhood Church sits in a shady neighborhood of a major metropolitan city. The church hosts two worship services every Sunday, has a very active youth group, and is involved in many of the social ministries happening in Major City.

For eleven years our church nested a school for children with special needs, until they outgrew our facility. Throughout those eleven years, I hoped that we could convey a sense of welcome to these families who faced tremendous physical, emotional, mental and, in many cases, financial stress. Not one family from the school ever visited our church on a Sunday morning. We tried offering a few combined activities, but I only remember one family coming to an Easter egg hunt. I often wondered what more we could have done, but at the same time I also wonder what we *would* have done if a family had shown up for Sunday School. We would have been very poorly equipped.

But we've been working hard, and word has slowly spread that children of all abilities are welcome here.

The Event

Jeremiah is a first grader with special needs. He has Greig's Syndrome, causing him to be prone to seizures and migraine headaches. His fine motor skill development is several years behind his peers and because of the internal structure of his hands, there are some things he will never be able to do. My youngest son has been serving as his Sunday School buddy for over two years, but on this particular Sunday we had asked a church member, Madeline, to fill in. She was looking forward to being with Jeremiah, as she is friends with his mother, and wanted to get to know him better.

On this particular Sunday, Jeremiah's first grade class would be coming to the drama/storytelling room to explore the story of creation. I was the teacher for this workshop and had planned a variety of hands on activities for this age group, including an outdoor seed scavenger hunt.

We had a full class. We had barely begun our first game when Madeline gathered Jeremiah up and took him out of the room. I wondered if maybe they had gone to the bathroom. We went on with the class, and I was expecting them to return. We had a wonderful time outdoors gathering seeds and delighting in the diversity we discovered. With about five minutes left, Madeline and Jeremiah returned. The children, aware that he had missed out, voluntarily began offering him a variety of seeds from their collections. The class ended with a group prayer.

After class, Madeline told me that we needed a new plan for Jeremiah. She said he either needed to be moved back to kindergarten (he is already seven and a half years old) or that we needed to create a separate class for children with special needs. Since there was not much time to discuss this—I needed to get ready for the 11:00 service—I listened to her concerns and told her I really appreciated her feedback and wanted to talk about this on Monday.

The next day, Madeline and I sat down to discuss the previous morning. I asked her to describe what had transpired, and why she had taken Jeremiah out so quickly. She thought he was being disruptive and/or that he was unhappy and decided to remove him from the situation. She feared that if he got upset he might have a seizure. (He had had a migraine the night before). I was able to talk with her about what my hopes had been and how I had designed a very "active" lesson plan with Jeremiah and the other first graders in mind. She was able to acknowledge that it was her fear of Jeremiah having a seizure in front of the other children, combined with her fear of him being disruptive that prompted her to remove him. She had assumed that, since we were in the storytelling room, there would be a high expectation for him to sit and listen, which she knew would be difficult for him.

REFLECTION

Viki Matson

Theological Questions

This case surfaces the following questions as starting points for theological reflection: *How are we to regard human difference? How does God regard human difference? Are people with disabilities created as fully and completely in God's image as those who are not disabled? What does wholeness/health/ salvation mean to one who lives with a disabling condition? How might the church model, in our structures and our practices, a different consciousness of ability and disability.*

Now that we have some questions named we have a place to start. We have something to respond to. What is the next step?

Sources for Theologizing

Scripture

This case study is entitled "Fearfully and Wonderfully Made," so if we wanted to plant our theological reflection in the soil of scripture we might give consideration to Psalm 139, from which the title came. Psalm 139 is an account of one creature's intimate relationship with the God who made them. It speaks of a God who "formed my inward parts" and who "knit me together in my mother's womb," a God intimately involved in the creation of each creature. With this in mind, it is very difficult to support the view that people with disabilities are *less than*. We would begin to be on thin ice if, after a careful study of this text, we maintained that some of us are more fearfully and wonderfully made than others. Encountering this text even prompted one man, the father of a child with multiple disabilities, to paraphrase the text in this provocative way:

> For you formed my inward parts *with Down syndrome;*
> you knitted me together in my mother's womb *without eyes.*
> I praise you, for I am fearfully and wonderfully made *with cognitive challenges.*
> Wonderful are your works *in creating me without limbs;*
> my soul knows it very well *though my ears will never hear a sound.*
> My frame was not hidden from you *as you made me with Apert syndrome,*
> when I was being made in secret *with autism,*
> intricately woven in the depths of the earth *without Hexosaminidase A.*
> Your eyes saw my unformed substance *with spina bifida;*
> in your book were written, every one of them,
> the days that were formed for me *with cerebral palsy,*
> when as yet there was none of them.[3]

3. Knight, "Is God Sovereign?"

Persons looking to scripture for clarity about what to believe and how to live regarding persons with disabilities find in this psalm a manifesto for embracing difference of all kinds as actually being a part of God's intention.

DOCTRINE

Alternatively, we might focus our reflection around a particular doctrine. In this case it seems appropriate to reflect upon the doctrine of creation and to wonder anew whether or not *all* of creation is, in fact, *good*. One might be inclined to think that occasionally creation is flawed or defective, and to conclude that some parts of creation are better, or more whole than others. It does not take much imagination to see how this assumption has led to all manner of discrimination, judgment, even genocide, against whole categories of people. This thinking is fraught with problems as it soon becomes clear that one's prejudices can become regrettably entwined with one's claims about God.

I would suggest that to claim that all creation is good, and that God's Spirit hovers near the process, necessarily means that one must have equal regard for all human beings, regardless of the ways in which they are different. God has engaged in a wildly diverse project in creating humankind, and God has declared that all of it is good. We fail to honor God when we create essential distinctions among ourselves. (Another possible pathway for reflection might be to explore what it means to be created in God's image, and to consider whether or not people with disabilities are God inspired, literally animated with God's breath.)

HERMENEUTICAL LENS

Yet another approach might be to employ a particular hermeneutical lens. Liberation theologians from many contexts have taught us that God does not operate by the same hierarchies of power and privilege by which we tend to organize human life. They claim that God not only has equal regard, but also *a preferential option for* those who have been outcast. Could this be true for people with disabilities, as well? Might the perspectives of liberation theologians help us clarify our own commitments toward people with disabilities?

I would suggest that considering this case study through a liberation lens might lead one to conclude that people with disabilities are not the problem, but rather the structure, architecture and processes around which much of life is organized have become impediments for a significant number of God's people. A liberation lens opens to a critical reflection, and even a bit of social analysis, about whether or not the ways of human beings are actually the ways of God.

Implications for Practice

It is clear from these brief reflections that theology informs practice. If I claim that all of us are fearfully and wonderfully made—a part of God's good creation—and that those who are usually excluded are perhaps even **preferentially regarded by God, then my practice of interacting with the** students in the Sunday School class described in this case will look very different than Madeline's. I learned from this reflection that I cannot have someone serve as a buddy without proper training. I cannot assume that even religious professionals are sensitized to persons with disabilities. Next time I would hope to embody God's love for Jeremiah by asking Madeline to teach the class while I served as Jeremiah's buddy, with an eye toward cultivating a cadre of teachers I would trust with any student. I also view my teaching of this Sunday School class as s long-term project in sensitizing the temporarily able-bodied students to the ways in which Jeremiah is different, in hopes of increasing their compassion toward him.

With such theological reflection, one has a solid starting point for evaluating and crafting ecclesial practices and rituals. Once a community has fully embraced the way in which God regards those with disabilities, every aspect of a community's life can be re-assessed to insure that realities mirror commitments. Everything from architecture and doorway sizes to use of bulletins, observance of silence and the role of ushers can be thought in light of our awareness of our theological beliefs. The unending circle of action and reflection that marks our unique process continues, as theology informs our practice and our practice expresses our theological claims.

REFLECTION

Christian Scharen

The context is Neighborhood Church, a church tucked away on a tree-lined street, but vital. With today's headline-grabbing focus on declining

mainline church attendance and increasing numbers of people discon-
necting from organized religion, we might be tempted to quickly dismiss
Neighborhood Church as unsexy, the kind of faith community we assume
will be "left behind" in the shifting lines of spirituality in the United States.
Yet listening carefully, details about the church—two services every Sunday, a "very active" youth group, and involvement in "many of the social
ministries" in the city—all point to a flourishing faith community. Further
confirmation of their vitality comes from the fact that the church hosted a
school for children with special needs for over a decade, only ending the
relationship because of the growth of the school.

The case's details highlight something of the theological commitments
of this congregation: a care for and deep commitment to youth, especially
those who need extra support, and an extension of this care to broader social concerns in the city. What are the explicit theological roots of this commitment? The title of the case hints that biblical affirmations of the wonder
of people—all people—matters here. While Psalm 139 is never mentioned
in the case, its title, "Fearfully and Wonderfully Made" comes from it.

The case is about an event during Sunday School—that is, during an
activity for youth that is one of the key activities of the congregation. The
situation revolves around the participation of a young boy, Jeremiah, with
Greig's Syndrome. While the disease affects people differently, in Jeremiah's
case it causes seizures and migraine headaches, as well as delayed motor-
skill development. The obvious though indirect connection to the school
for children with special needs, and this particular special needs boy in
Sunday School, deepen our sense of the church's commitment and welcome
to youth. Additionally, the student who wrote the case is closely connected
to Jeremiah. His youngest son has been a Sunday School buddy for over
two years. Being a buddy is an embodied symbol of care for another, of
attending to Jeremiah and giving him space to be more fully, safely present.
It is a posture of love, one shown in Jesus' own formation of his disciples
when he knelt at their feet with a towel and basin of water.

While the specific Sunday School lessons no doubt teach good things,
this living parable likely teaches the gospel to both buddies, and to their
whole class.

The specific event described took place on a day when Jeremiah's regular buddy was unavailable and another church member, Madeline, filled in.
A friend of Jeremiah's mother, she looked forward to getting to know him
better through this substitute buddy assignment. The case writer, also the

teacher of the class, had planned a session focused on the story of creation with hands-on, active learning that Jeremiah could easily participate in. But despite this care in planning, Madeline feared Jeremiah could not handle the lesson and removed him for most of the hour. Upon their return, the students showed their own compassion and connection with Jeremiah by offering him seeds from their collection gathered during the hour's outdoor activity. Madeline rather abruptly stated that Sunday School needed a new plan for Jeremiah—either he should be moved down to a lower-aged class or they should create a class for those with special needs. After listening carefully to her concerns, but unable to take time to discuss the matter further right then, the teacher made plans to reconnect with Madeline the next day.

When they did reconnect a day later, he carefully set a context for hearing her experience, rather than asking more about the solutions she had led with the previous day. What had transpired, he asked, that caused her to leave with Jeremiah? Here, a kind of combined compassion and non-judgmental response grounded his effort to listen, sending to her a signal that she could pause, exhale, show up, and be real about her experience of the situation. It turns out she had been anxious for Jeremiah, partly because of her judgment that he was not happy at the beginning of class, and partly because of her prior knowledge that he'd had a migraine the night before. As the teacher listened to Madeline, he learned that her abrupt action was provoked by her fear of Jeremiah having a seizure combined with her worry that the lesson would require him to sit still.

The various players in the situation show the genuineness of their compassion and care all the way through the case. The implicit theological grounding of the congregation's practices of care for another, of making space for the other to appear as a full self, could be construed as a claim that everyone is a 'child of God' in Baptismal terms. The challenge here seemed mostly to be lack of adequate preparation for Madeline so that she would know what to expect rather than be driven by her anxiety and fears. More preparation for the buddy role would have allowed her to be at peace with and for Jeremiah during the Sunday School hour. Despite this oversight, though, the case generally demonstrates that people at Neighborhood Church were engaged in a spiritual discipline of listening, caring, and making a special effort to be in relationship to one whose needs might put him on the margins.

QUESTION FOR DISCUSSION

1. If theology and practice are genuinely circular, as Matson claims, with practice informing theology as well as the reverse, then how might we reflect further on Madeline's practice of protecting Jeremiah from a seizure? Is the impulse to prevent a child's suffering also grounded in some theological claim?

BIBLIOGRAPHY

Bourdieu, Pierre. *In Other Words: Essays Towards a Reflexive Sociology.* Translated by Matthew Adamson. Palo Alto, CA: Stanford University Press, 1990.

Dillard, Annie. *Pilgrim at Tinker Creek.* New York: Harper & Row, 1974.

Knight, John. "Is God Sovereign over Human Disability?" *desiringGod.* May 6, 2010. http:www.desiringgod.org/articles/is-god-sovereign-over-human-disability. Used with permission.

3

To Give or Not to Give?

Nannette Banks and Tracy Hartman

INTRODUCTION

Banks:

I CHOSE TO USE Joe Holland and Peter Henroit's *Social Analysis: Linking Faith and Justice.*[1] Their model is represented by a circle that they call the "pastoral circle." The image indicates a continual process, which I find useful when trying to unravel the historical webs of politics, race, culture and class in a case (not to mention in daily life). The model also allows me to be present and attentive as I work through my personal reaction into a more critical social analysis.

The Holland-Henriot pastoral circle has four "moments": *Insertion*, the geographically located experiences of ordinary people; *Social Analysis*, which locates experiences in a broader picture of causes and consequences; *Theological Reflection*, which brings to bear the resources of the faith upon the analyzed experience; and *Pastoral Planning*, which is decision and action for the short- and long-term. Since decision and action themselves usher in new experiences, the circle continues.[2]

1. Holland and Henriot, *Social Analysis.*
2. Ibid., 7–10.

Holland and Henriot's model emphasizes the systemic unity of personal experience, facts, issues, and social theories. Neither purely pragmatic nor purely issue-driven, it threads them together. As they wrote, "To stop with anecdotes, to concentrate only on issues, obscures the comprehensive systemic picture."[3] Therefore I begin my reflection with an anecdote from my own personal experience, moving immediately from that experience into a social analysis of the issues embedded in it and in the case, and from there on to theological reflection framed by the question, 'What can we do to heal, redeem, and liberate?'. I conclude with concrete action suggestions imagined not only for the community of the case but for readers as well.

Hartman:

The Whiteheads' model of theological reflection provides an appropriate framework for this case.[4] In this model, a presenting issue or challenge is placed within the context of a triangular relationship among three points of analysis: *The Surrounding Culture*—which can include economic, political, and social issues influencing the case; *Experience*—of both the individual believer and the community; and *The Religious Tradition*—which includes Scripture and the traditions of both the local and global contexts. As the reader will see, these points overlap, and material contained in one section of analysis could easily be placed in another. Ultimately, the integration of insights gained from reflecting on all three points leads to effective praxis in the future.

Not surprisingly, Nannette and I both gravitated to the larger issues that undergird this case, especially issues of race and class and culture. We both situated ourselves vis à vis the case as reflectors shaped directly and personally by these issues, with Nannette making her situation most explicit. Both of us noticed things in the case that the other did not see because of our respective social locations. The pairing of our reflections in this chapter thus gives readers an especially helpful demonstration of how multiple perspectives on the same case enrich reflection, and the resultant emphasis on the importance of perspective adds yet a further layer to the way readers might reflect on the case, itself a case about perspective. The angle and selectivity of our perspective—or, if you will, our blind spots—deeply influence the meaning we make of another's experience.

3. Ibid., 10.
4. Whitehead and Whitehead, *Method in Ministry*, 6.

THE CASE

Context

St. Luke's Parish is a wealthy, largely white congregation in a major metropolitan area in the South. The beautiful sanctuary fills to capacity each Sunday with about 1,200 persons in the worshiping congregation. There's a real sense of concern for the larger community within which it is located, even as it struggles to relate meaningfully with its downtown location and the population that finds its home there. Most commute to the church to participate on Sunday mornings. The lay leaders of the church also serve on the boards of a number of non-profits in the community. Pastor Williams and his staff of six women and men are deeply committed and have been extremely welcoming to me for this field education experience.

Event

Gregory is an elderly black man. He is homeless and stands out in this very white congregation. Nevertheless, Gregory has made St. Luke's his parish community. Or so it was.

The first week that I came to St. Luke's I met Gregory in the bathroom, where he asked me for money. I sensed that this was familiar conversational ground for Gregory and I made it clear that I wanted to get to know him, not just give him money. Moreover, I didn't have my wallet on me. When I later asked about Gregory, I was met with a look of concern and a complicated story.

Gregory had made St. Luke's his parish, yes, but there were questions regarding his motives. There had been complaints regarding his requests for money. A few women complained that they felt unsafe around him. Others thought him manipulative, as he preferred to ask people directly for help instead of going through the "appropriate channels" where the money could be most efficiently apportioned and monitored. Somewhere along the way, the grumblings of other parishioners prompted the clergy to ask Gregory not to beg on Sundays. "Come any other day of the week and meet with our ministry leaders" they asked, "just don't ask people for help on Sundays." To ensure that Gregory understood, the clergy asked him to read and sign a contract spelling out the agreement that he could come on Sundays as long as he didn't ask anyone for money.

Gregory persistently ignored their requests and ignored the contract that he signed. He showed up a few more times and asked for money, this time cunningly writing his request on a napkin and then showing the napkin to folks in passing. He'd been given numerous warnings, the story went, and he refused to reform. So when I asked about Gregory, it was the last straw. The church leadership asked Gregory to refrain from coming to St. Luke's for one year.

The following week, the lectionary text was Luke 14. Jesus says, "When you give a luncheon or a dinner, do not invite your friends or your brothers or your relatives or rich neighbors, in case they may invite you in return, and you would be repaid. But when you give a banquet, invite the poor, the crippled, the lame, and the blind. And you will be blessed, because they cannot repay you, for you will be repaid at the resurrection of the righteous." I couldn't help but struggle with the irony and the difficulty of the situation.

REFLECTION

Nannette Banks

Insertion

It became vivid all over again the moment I read Gregory's case. I hadn't realized the feeling was still lurking. But I had once felt just like Gregory, being treated as the 'other.' Race and class had been neck and neck in the experience, no clear lead, just side by side they'd trotted.

> "You must work here," were the words she spoke to me as I stood on the grounds of one of the oldest Christian institutions in the nation, one that in 2010 was still struggling to break the color and class barrier. I, an African American woman with two graduate degrees, ordination and a world traveler, was assumed to be 'the help' by an older white woman who was now backing away and nervously laughing. "No ma'am," (maybe I should not have said that, but my upbringing prevailed to respect my elders) "I am here as a fellow in the program enjoying the same lectures, preachers and fine arts activities as you are." She disappeared around the corner and I turned on my heels with a bit of labored breathing, asking God, *"Why am I here? This is the second time this week someone has assumed that I am 'the help' even though not even the cleaning people here are African American or folks of color."*

I was Gregory, in that recalled moment.

Social Analysis

It appears that, like the elderly white woman in my memory, parishioners were wondering how or whether Gregory belonged there, questioning his motives and reporting a lack of safety because of his presence. I am sure their body language relayed their unease even if they smiled all the while reaching into their pockets to grant his request. Did Gregory assume a particular posture as he entered the wealthy white church? Did the congregation assume a particular posture when he entered? Many parishioners labeled Gregory as manipulative but continued to give money when he asked, and then complained. None of them confronted Gregory directly, probably out of a fear of being labeled racist, classist or simply unchristian. Such are the caricatured roles of what it means to be black in the South and what it means to be white in the South. These historical postures have a way of manifesting themselves knowingly or unknowingly. What really struck me was that the white intern thought he already knew Gregory's story: *"I sensed that this was familiar conversational ground for Gregory and I made it clear that I wanted to get to know him, not just give him money."* I suspect these historical tensions and postures were what caused Gregory's story to feel familiar to the intern.

> Let the Church discover and identify itself with groups of people that suffer because of unjust situations, and who have no way of making themselves heard. The Church should be the voice of those who have no one. The Church must discover these groups and identify herself with them. Here is the modern way of the Cross, the way of Christian responsibility.[5]

A large southern, white, wealthy church. That description alone conjures thoughts of the powerful—the decision makers and the 1%. It is clear that the leadership is well connected to agencies within the community by virtue of serving as board members. Their service may be to assist the least of these in gaining access to what they need, or it may be self-serving. The description of the church is also laced with the potential for racism, classism, and exclusivism. There in the midst of an urban neighborhood this church stands. Who is 'neighbor' to them? Who is 'community'? In some

---

5. Emilio Castro, cited in Cone, *Black Theology*, 62.

urban churches, they are outside the church walls and in others, within. The difference is critical because passion, purpose, sacrifice, and hospitality come along with who you identify as your neighbor, your community. Churches represent themselves differently depending on whether they acknowledge that the community lies inside as well as outside their walls.

Theological Reflection

> "We must face the sad fact that at eleven o'clock on Sunday morning when we stand to sing "In Christ there is no East or West," we stand in the most segregated hour of America." - *Reverend Dr. Martin Luther King, Jr.*[6]

We all are likely to agree with the above MLK quote, but it is still an arresting statement. Arresting because it forces us to acknowledge the ways in which the politics of classism and racism erect borders within the lives of congregations. As soon as the intern saw Gregory in the bathroom and "sensed" this was familiar conversational ground for Gregory, a border went up. The intern was unable to cross it and imagine Gregory having an immediate need not linked to some ongoing "ask" campaign. Instead of taking the moment to offer Gregory coffee and get to know him, the intern instead protested that he did not have his wallet on him. Not a fully honest message, considering what his next move was: going to the pastoral staff. Yet another border creeps up. This one caused by the assumption that someone else would know the truth about Gregory's story better than Gregory himself. After all, why ask others instead of asking Gregory directly? It is a bold move to question someone's need on the spot, but their begging might be just the invitation to do so.

Wasn't that the entry point for Jesus's understanding the need of the blind beggar on the side of the road? *As Jesus approached Jericho, a blind man was sitting by the roadside begging. . .He called out, "Jesus, Son of David, have mercy on me!" Those who led the way rebuked him and told him to be quiet. . .And Jesus stopped, and commanded him to be brought to him; and when he came near, he asked him, "What do you want me to do for you?"* The man had kept on begging much to the chagrin of those who benefited from

6. Martin Luther King, Jr., "Remaining Awake through a Great Revolution," a sermon delivered at the National Cathedral in Washington, DC, March 31, 1968, in Holloran and Carson, *Knock at Midnight*, 201.

the beggar remaining the beggar. He asked for mercy until Jesus heard him across the border and invited him closer (Luke 18:35–42).

Those who rebuked the beggar were attempting to maintain the status quo. Many in the crowd were those who had followed Jesus and had even worked with Jesus in various capacities—witnessing the miracles, the healings and the transformations. Many of the crowd dwellers were direct beneficiaries themselves. Yet they were still unable to imagine that this beggar, this outsider from Jericho, deserved access to Jesus. Unable to imagine that this beggar had a story any different from any other beggar they had known. Unable to imagine that the beggar had hopes to be more than a beggar. Unable to imagine that the beggar had a story besides the one concocted in their heads which was shaped by stereotypes about race, class and religion. The "rebukers" were uncomfortable and simply wanted him to go away, relieving them of their social and communal responsibility to know their neighbor and to assist the widow, the orphan and the poor. Their subconscious behavior aided in the perpetuation of a permanent underclass.

The rebukers' message: All are not welcome to access the abundance of God. If your rung is too low on the social and economic ladder in society, you are not welcome. To access the Divine, you must have yourself together and, besides, there is not enough room for us all. But Jesus called the man to him and asked him a direct question, an uncomfortable question, an awkward question: *"What do you want me to do for you?"* I am sure this ushered in a deafening silence, with many wondering what the beggar's response would be. Fortune? Fame? Instead, it was this: to be made whole. Something we all are seeking, as we all are broken.

The larger theological themes in this case border our daily living. They are our unwillingness to reflect deeply on encounters that leave us initially feeling uneasy, our resistance toward thinking outside of the box in such moments, and our reproduction of that which we say we abhor—the endless list of injustices, inequalities, and perpetuations of the status quo.

Pastoral Planning

"It is impossible to dialogue if I do not perceive my own brokenness, my own ignorance, my own lack of wisdom. It is a sheer act of arrogance to enter into a discussion with the purpose of convincing others that I possess the truth and will bestow it upon them. In true dialogue, neither perceives the other as ignorant nor themselves as the font of wisdom. They are persons coming together to learn what they do not know."—Regina Coll, CSJ[7]

"Why am I here?" We each have a cultural frame of reference. The race, religion, and class narratives that impact our daily living mean that none of us sees another without seeing through these lenses. Unfortunately, we as pastors, preachers, supervisors, interns, and congregants are not exempt. Woven into our stories are historical tensions and posturing, and when we feel that the 'other' has invaded our space, we often act and speak in ways that leave someone with the question "Why am I here?"

St. Luke's will need to revisit their mission and vision to be reminded of their purpose and their call to be the church in people's lives. This call will tug on their compassion and care for humanity as they remember that God's grace and mercy are available to all. It will not mean that Gregory is let off the hook and his actions condoned, but neither were his actions worthy of expulsion from the church and a community of believers. Continued theological reflection, not only with the intern but throughout the leadership in general, will be key. If they are willing to reflect on and pray about their decision and to consider it differently, they might invite Gregory back for a conversation with the pastoral staff about his experience of them. They might ask themselves about their experience of him. Eventually, he might participate on an advisory board within the church that includes lay members, pastoral staff, and community agency folks to review issues like the ones emerging in this case.

It is imperative that we all train ourselves in cultural sensitivity, anti-racism and diversity issues.[8] This is ongoing, tough work but well worth it. We are all called to ensure that all are welcome to access the abundance and goodness of God, and that no one be forced to answer for why they are there.

---

7. Coll, *Supervision of Ministry Students*, 56.

8. Tools such as the Workplace Big Five Profile, 360, and the Intercultural Development Inventory are helpful in gaining a more honest view of our leadership styles.

REFLECTION

Tracy Hartman

Cultural Issues

The cultural issues of poverty, homelessness, class, and race are all relevant to this case. All of us are acculturated to behave in certain ways. Research by psychologist Jennifer Eberhardt has shown that stereotypes shape what we see. Specifically, her research studies have shown that stereotypical thinking or assumptions can impact whether we detect a threat when looking at an individual.[9] Accordingly, in this case we might assume that Southern white parishioners like those at St. Luke's would primarily see someone like Gregory as a threat or an 'other' in need of assistance rather than as an equal member of the family of faith. If Gregory is indeed viewed as a threat or as 'other,' the congregation might benefit from exploring whether their mindset is due to Gregory's persistent requests for money, from lingering perceptions of African Americans as less than equal in Southern culture, or both.

From social psychology we also receive the theory that humans will persist in behaviors that reward them in some way. Perhaps Gregory continues to beg simply because people continue to give him money! If his behavior wasn't bringing desired results, after all, he wouldn't likely persist week after week. But then we have to wonder why the parishioners continue to respond positively to his requests for assistance. Gregory's situation does not appear to be changing in the long term, so how much are parishioners really helping? Their 'reward' for giving Gregory money over and over again must stem from something else. Perhaps they would feel guilty for *not* responding, and so giving eases their guilt. Or perhaps it meets their need to make just enough of a difference so that they can avoid engaging the deeper social and cultural issues that lead to poverty and homelessness.

The case does not tell us whether or not St. Luke's has shown any commitment as a parish to dealing with the larger societal and systemic issues that perpetuate homelessness and poverty, or whether they have been content instead to limit their efforts to meeting short term needs. If the latter, they are continuing, perhaps unknowingly, to perpetuate a cycle

9. See Eberhardt et al., "Seeing Black," 879–93. Eberhardt's work gained renewed attention in the Fall of 2014 as many US communities questioned the perceptions of Black men held by police officers.

of dependency of the poor upon the non-poor. Churches are not alone in struggling with this problem of poverty. Non-profit organizations and local state and federal agencies also face the question of whether to work for long-term change or immediate assistance. Wider collaboration among organizations, agencies, and churches might therefore be the best way to bring about sustained change.

Personal Experience

Reflection on personal experience can yield fruitful insights into behaviors and reactions in a given ministry setting. The case does not tell us **where the field education student grew up, but if he is from the North**, or from suburbia, Southern culture and urban church life might be totally new experiences for him. If he were raised in need rather than comfort, he might be more familiar with people like Gregory than St. Luke's parishioners are. If his family and home church modeled a different response than theirs to poverty and homelessness, all the more would he react with surprise and discomfort to their way of treating Gregory. If such issues have been dealt with in his seminary course work, he might be more prepared for his encounter with Gregory than if they have not. All of his past personal experiences are sources of knowledge for him.

In the present, the case describes the student's report of his conversation as the "last straw" leading to Gregory's expulsion from St. Luke's. The student would understandably feel guilty that his report led to disciplinary action for Gregory. The situation became charged with emotion on all sides. In the future, therefore, some coaching for the student on how to respond to emotionally charged circumstances with emotional intelligence could be extremely beneficial for his long-term success in ministry

Scripture and Tradition

Turning to Scripture, the student's response to the lectionary text from Luke 14 for the following Sunday seems appropriate. This passage naturally brought the issue with Gregory to a head for the student because parallels between Gregory and the passage's "poor, crippled, and lame" were apt. And yet, the student still appears to miss something in the text. There is a difference between *inviting* the poor *in* and merely *responding* or *reacting* to their requests for assistance. If the poor were routinely invited to the

39

"banquet," after all, would they still need to beg? Other gospel passages similarly speak of Jesus' compassionate response to the poor in a way that contrasts with the behavior at St. Luke's. When the disciples seek to keep the children (Mark 10:13–16) and blind Bartimaeus (Luke 10:46–52) from Jesus, he rebukes the disciples and welcomes the disenfranchised. Even when Jesus experienced what we now call 'compassion fatigue,' he ministered to the needs of those around him.

There are also cases of begging and nagging being rewarded in Scripture. In Luke 18, it is the persistent widow who is granted justice. In the story of the Syrophoenician woman, we see growth and change in Jesus as he first rebukes the woman but then heals her daughter. The woman is persistent in her plea, and she is not afraid to offer her own rebuke of Jesus. Even though Jesus demeans the woman in the beginning of this story, eventually, like all others that Jesus encounters, he treats her with respect and basic human dignity. The situation at St. Luke's would change if Gregory were treated as a full partner in the gospel and the life of the church. In the same way that Jesus learned from the Syrophoenician woman, St. Luke's needs to learn from Gregory.

As faithful practitioners, we must balance these texts with others that give us a different view. In the feeding miracles, Jesus sat the crowd down in groups and had the disciples distribute the food in an orderly manner. The New Testament also tells us that deacons in the early church were elected to bring equity and justice to the church's service ministries. Such texts suggest that St. Luke's may have acted wisely when developing policies and procedures to guide their benevolence programs. Even though Gregory's own preferred approach was to ask people personally for money on Sunday mornings, and even though the way St. Luke's administered its aid might have made him feel demeaned or uncomfortable, their approach might represent a desire not just for order but also for justice by distributing their resources equitably among all who ask.

Beyond traditions represented by Scripture are traditions of the local parish, denomination, and wider community. Churches would normally do well to follow their own past patterns for dealing with persons like Gregory, assuming their choices have had integrity. Sometimes the larger denominational body has guidelines and policies that dictate the work of the local church, and if these policies prove adequate they should carry weight. Also relevant are the ways that other churches in the same urban area are dealing with the issue of begging. Some towns and cities try to establish ways of responding to begging that everyone will practice in common. Finally, as mentioned above, there are surely non-profit agencies in the city with which St. Luke's could forge partnerships in addressing the larger systemic issues of poverty and homelessness in their city. Such partnerships represent both gains and losses for individual churches. St. Luke's might gain a sense of solidarity with others in tackling the large problems while losing a sense of immediacy that comes from helping individuals like Gregory one-on-one. But St. Luke's might do well to consider what it would mean for them to engage at the level of social change and not just charity alone.

Future Praxis

St. Luke's frustration with Gregory is understandable in many ways, yet their response seems at odds with the heart of the gospel. Is Gregory equally frustrated with St. Luke's? One wonders if anyone ever asked Gregory for his thoughts about his own begging. Hopefully theological reflection on the issues involved would lead St. Luke's to view Gregory as a full member of their body and to include him in future praxis.

QUESTIONS FOR DISCUSSION

1. Many reflectors find it difficult to make the move "from the anecdotal to the analytical," as Holland and Henriot put it,[10] and then back again to the anecdotal. What makes these movements so hard? How do you overcome the difficulty?

2. Can you think of a time when another reflector exposed your own blind spot? How did the exposure inform your further reflection and, ultimately, your practice of ministry?

---

10. Holland and Henriot, *Social Analysis,* 10.

BIBLIOGRAPHY

Coll, Regina, CSJ. *Supervision of Ministry Students*. Collegeville, MN: Liturgical, 1992.

Cone, James H. *Black Theology and Black Power*. New York: Harper & Row, 1969.

Eberhardt, Jennifer L. et al., "Seeing Black: Race, Crime and Visual Processing." *Journal of Personality and Social Psychology* 87 (2004) 876–893.

Holland, Joe, and Peter Henriot, SJ. *Social Analysis: Linking Faith and Justice*. Rev. and enl. ed. Maryknoll, NY: Orbis, 1983.

Holloran, Peter, and Clayborne Carson, eds. *A Knock at Midnight: Inspiration from the Great Sermons of Reverend Martin Luther King, Jr.* New York: Warner, 2000.

Whitehead, James D. and Evelyn Eaton Whitehead. *Method in Ministry: Theological Reflection and Christian Ministry*. Rev. ed. Lanham, MD: Sheed & Ward, 1995.

4

Robert in the Clutch of Grief

Annette Brownlee and Emily Click

INTRODUCTION

Click:

I EMPLOY A FORMAT for reflection that has evolved from Patricia O'Connell Killen and John de Beer's *The Art of Theological Reflection*.[1] I begin by naming the *feelings* of the primary actor in the case. Next I let the feelings evoke *images* that capture the meaning of the action. The most useful images go beyond literally illustrating what happened. Often the most instructive images encapsulate theological or personal meaning embedded in the arc of events. Next, I discuss *theological issues* that might relate to the dynamics at work in the case. Finally, I identify how this reflective cycle informs *future ministerial action*.

Students often write cases about incidents that they feel did not go particularly well. These kinds of cases offer special potential for learning about dependency on God's power and presence, and about options for moral human action. Even in the act of depicting a situation that has no obvious solution, students develop new disciplines of searching for meaning. Insight emerges from quagmires where motives, purposes, feelings

---

1. Killen and de Beer, *The Art of Theological Reflection*, 88.

and theological meanings seem hidden from view. In practicing a method of reflection that focuses on the motivations of actors, they cultivate both flexibility in interpreting ministerial action and humility in their own ministerial leadership.

In my own work, I prefer to use the term *ministerial reflection* because it encompasses more than 'theological reflection.' Ministers must correlate theological insights with a host of other concerns when they design faithful responses to incidents. Ministerial reflection, then, takes into account the interplay among multiple levels of the dynamics in a case study incident. For example, the contemplation of personal, individual feelings might be informed by consideration of organizational problems or interpersonal issues. Some cases might require that legal and ethical issues be taken into consideration in the design of theologically informed responses. With respect to this case, "Robert's" own emotions both affected and were affected by the fact that he was one member of a multiple clergy staff.

I wrote my reflection assuming the voice of "Robert."

Brownlee:

My approach is influenced by the work of Patricia O'Connell Killen and John de Beer on theological reflection, the work of Andrew Purves on reconstructing pastoral theology from a Christological perspective, and the work of George Lindbeck on post-liberal theology.[2] It is designed to recast the formation of Christian leaders into a reflection on ministerial competencies *in light of* a reflection on the church's ministry as participation in Christ's ministry.[3] My ultimate goal is to help students frame the pastoral care of the church in light of God's care of us. In such an approach, Scripture is not correlated with propositional statements or universal experience. The meaning of Scripture is located within it and the world it describes. The bridge between Scripture and the present is the ministry of the church, through its communal life and practices. For the purposes of this process, Christ's ministry is defined as God's ongoing actions (as described in Scripture) through the Spirit for the sake of the world.

I have reflectors follow a four-step process that begins with a deep description of what is going on in the case,[4] and secondly moves into

2. Ibid.; Purves, *Pastoral Theology*; Lindbeck, *Nature of Doctrine*.

3. This is Purves' main argument.

4. Specific questions I might ask in Step One include: What is happening? Who is

exploring the heart of the case through the lens of Scripture.[5] They then explore responses to Christ's ministry, as named through God's actions in the Scripture passages identified in the second step.[6] Finally, in step four, reflectors imagine ways they might participate in Christ's ministry.[7]

My goal is to engage in what Killen has called "mid-range reflection" in *all* four steps.[8] Reflectors ponder their own experiences, the ongoing ministry of Jesus Christ, and reconceive of their responses or actions as participation in Christ's ministry. To reconceive their ministries this way requires "a slowing down," in which reflectors step into Scripture and Christ's ministry even as they do their own experience.[9]

My reflection is written in the form of a class discussion among MDiv students led by a facilitator.

THE CASE

Robert is a field education student who has been placed at Emmanuel, a multi-staff Episcopal (Anglican) church in an affluent neighborhood where he has no prior relationship to the congregation. Robert is happy to be working with the rector whom he perceives as a warm, emotionally available priest and leader. He hopes the rector will become a mentor.

On Sunday mornings Robert assumes various roles at the 8 and 10 a.m. services of Holy Communion: reading Scripture, chanting the Psalm, leading the Prayers of the People, assisting with the Holy Communion. The rector assigns him these roles during their weekly staff meetings, in

---

involved? What images speak to the heart of what is going on? If images are not forthcoming I try to capture in a sentence the tension which is at the heart of the case.

5. Step Two questions: What passages come to mind as you think about the case? How is the heart of the matter described in there? What parts of the scriptural description are new to you, as you think about the case? What is the form and shape of Christ's ministry in these various parts of Scripture as known through God's actions?

6. Step Three questions: What might be the possible reactions of participants to the Christ's ministry here? Why? What is going on in your response to God's actions here? Why? Where is it hard to follow Christ here?

7. Step Four questions: How is Christ's ministry here interpreted through the communal life of the church and its practices? What are the means of grace God has given this church to participate in Christ's ministry? What is the church's role? What is not? What is your role? What is not? What do you need to take responsibility for?

8. Killen "Midrange Reflection."

9. Killen and de Beer, *The Art of Theological Reflection*.

advance of that Sunday's service. Later in the term Robert will preach a few times. He hasn't preached yet.

During his second week in the placement, Robert learns that his favorite uncle has recently been diagnosed with cancer. Robert is devastated and shares this news with the rector during their weekly supervision session. He explains that it is particularly devastating since this uncle and aunt are like surrogate parents to him. He tells the rector he just does not feel like he can continue on as usual with schoolwork.

A few weeks after the news of his uncle's cancer diagnosis, Robert is having a hard time engaging with his Sunday morning responsibilities. Due to his overall distress, he doesn't want to be at Emmanuel that day, at all. He wants to be with his uncle, or at least to be able to be at home in his room: able to think, feel, and talk with his family via FaceTime. During the staff meeting that week, Robert agreed to lead the Prayers of the People at the 10 a.m. service.

Between the services, when the clerical staff usually touches base, the rector finds Robert sitting in a small library by himself, curled up in a chair, and looking angry. The rector asks him if he is all right and Robert declares he just can't lead the prayers at the 10 a.m. service. He is too upset about his uncle and he wants to be left alone. The rector tells him he will find someone else to lead the prayers, but he expects Robert to be in the service.

During their supervisory hour the next week the rector tells Robert that he is disappointed in him for pulling out of leading the prayers and that it must not happen again. Robert is surprised at this disapproval, and can't understand what he did wrong. It seems very discouraging that the rector behaves in a way that seems to him to be lacking in pastoral sensitivity and grace.

REFLECTION

Emily Click

My number one question emerging from my case study is: *How do I become an authentic leader of worship even when I am subsumed in my own grief?* My experience on the Sunday I wrote about disclosed to me how reluctant I am to fake my faith. I did not want to lead the community prayers because I was filled with rage and fear. It seemed to me it would be blasphemy to pray when I felt alienated from God. I was unhappy when my supervisor nudged me toward leading anyway. I was relieved when he arranged for someone else to fill in. However, I have since learned something vital from thinking about how it would have gone if I could have just done it. I have realized that God can use even the reluctant leader in authentic ways, just as God receives gifts from every reluctant giver.

I was fused with my own feelings that Sunday. I am now embarrassed to reflect upon how childlike I must have appeared, curled up in the chair in the church library. My supervisor might well have seen me as a little kid cultivating his tantrum. At the time, however, I was simply unable to find myself. I was in such shock I could no longer get perspective on what was happening well enough even to hide in a more discrete location. My questions in that moment were: 'How can I be this person who no longer has Uncle Joe in his life?' 'How am I going to keep on going?' Since that Sunday, I have remembered my class on pastoral counseling and I now know for sure how many other people have lived through far worse situations. At the time, however, other people's experience made no difference to me. My own grief was all I could think about.

After that day, I began to doubt my capacity to serve not just in that moment, but also in the future. Before that day, it had all been academic. I knew that life could get really difficult at any point. I knew that lots of people suffered incapacitating grief. But what I knew were just statistics. This felt so unique, so tremendous, so disorienting. I began to doubt I could help anyone else if my own relatively normal loss was such a big deal. I began to wonder not only how I could learn to 'fake it' and lead prayers in difficult moments but also whether I was just a big fake when it came to relying on God. Is relying on God something I talk about from the pulpit but cannot really put into play when the going gets rough?

I had been so wrapped up in my own feelings that day I never even considered what it might be like for my supervisor when I was unable to lead prayers. It was only in our follow-up reflection time that I began to consider his feelings. He was surprised at my reluctance to do something I had promised to do. I think he also was put into a tough spot because I did not arrange my absence in advance. I realized later I also was expecting him to take care of me, when that was not his job, most certainly not in the middle of a busy Sunday morning. I guess my therapist might wonder if I was unconsciously trying to get him to fill in for my uncle. None of those things occurred to me at the time, of course. Now I realize there was a lot more going on than I had any idea of at the time.

An image has come to me in reflecting on my experience. I have this vivid picture of Lazarus' sisters pleading with Jesus. In fact, that whole story from John 11 has come alive. I can literally feel what Mary and Martha must have felt when Jesus delayed and their brother Lazarus died. The desperation, the disbelief that someone might be gone from this life—for me my uncle, for them their brother—is so clear to me. I know I am not alone. Jesus saw that look of loss, of soul-surrounding grief, in the eyes of his dear friends Mary and Martha. Jesus therefore knows my grief as well. It just came at me like lightning one day: when they pled with Jesus, it was of course an early model for our prayers. I now realize I would *not* be faking faith if I were to lead prayers in the midst of my own grief. I would be standing in the same holy space as the sisters of Lazarus!

It is sacred to stand before God filled with need. Sometimes as a pastoral leader I will stand in that place for others, and at other times my needs will flow right alongside theirs. When the image of Lazarus' sisters first filled my head, I began to ache inside with a need to pray. I realized I did not want to stay away from praying, either for myself or for others. When I compose prayers for others, I will attempt to recall that ache, so that the prayers will be authentic. I think prayers become inauthentic when we just sit around with nothing particular on our minds, and write something pretty to say out loud in the spot allotted for prayers in the worship. Authenticity matters to me, and I will try never to write great sounding prayers instead of those tethered to real life joy and sorrow.

I have come through this experience with a new level of understanding of how I must wrestle with my own inner struggles in order to be able to serve others. I want to be more careful with how I approach my role at the church, and not expect I can just hang out there as if I were in my pj's eating Cheerios. I realize now I have the kind of role that means dealing with difficult things so they inform but do not disable my ministry. I also want to be more careful about coordinating with my supervisor and future pastoral colleagues. Sunday morning is a high pressure time and I must imagine how my actions affect them. Before, I never felt like my actions had much of an impact on others. Now I realize that my grief, my love, and my faith—made stronger by the loss of my uncle—are full of meaning that I can share.

Annette Brownlee

Step 1: Reflection on the Specifics of the Case Study

Facilitator: Our first step is to do a deep description of what's going on in the case. Let's start by naming who is involved in this case as active participants and who are its passive participants.

Student A: Robert and the supervisor are active. I think the congregation itself is an active participant in this case because they were mentioned in the first paragraph.

Student B: I disagree about the congregation. I think what happened to Robert would have happened anywhere; in fact, his oblivion to the members of the congregation unfortunately renders them passive, whether or not they might have been a source of God's love and care for him.

What about Robert's aunt and uncle?

All: They are definitely participants in this case because their suffering is the source of Robert's anguish, but they are passive participants because they are distant.

Where is the turning point or key event in the case?

Student C: Robert's behavior in the library is key. Everything revolves around his collapse on that Sunday morning because the heart of the matter is a minister's ability to keep going while ministering to others.

Student D: I agree with you about the heart of the matter but that's why I actually think the supervisory hour the following week is the more important moment. It's in that hour that the contrast between supervisor and student becomes so stark. It's when Robert realizes with surprise that he had been expected to carry on that morning no matter what, with his supervisor allowing so little mercy for his reaction to his uncle's cancer, that the case comes to a head.

What do the participants' feelings, motivations, and reactions indicate to us about the heart of the matter in this case?

A: Robert is devastated by the news of his uncle's cancer and it renders him unsure of his abilities, unable to lead the prayers, and angry.

Angry?

A: Yes, I think when he's curled up in the library, his primary feeling is anger.

B: I think the primary feeling is fear—fear of loss and of his own inability to go on.

C: But his complete withdrawal from the congregation indicates to me quite a bit of anger.

Is there an image in this case that captures the heart of the matter?

D: When I imagine Robert withdrawn to the library, curled up, angry, and unwilling to lead the prayers, I get the image of a sulking child, trying to draw attention to himself.

Student E: Yes, there's a narcissistic element to his grief.

A: Oh, I don't know. I think you're being too harsh on Robert!

Do you have an alternative image?

A: No, I guess I can't come up with one.

Anybody else?

[Silence.]

Let's not force consensus around a key image. After all, we all have different responses to grief and we bring all of those to our interpretation of the case. I would note that while you all react differently to Robert's behavior, your energy is focused on his actions rather than any of the other participants in the case.

Step 2: Interpretation of the Heart of the Matter through the Lens of Scripture

Let's move to step two and interpret the heart of the matter through the lens of Scripture. You've identified the heart of the matter in this case as Robert's response to a loss. What scriptural texts describe human feelings or actions similar to that? Let's not just search for familiar or favorite passages but ones that describe God's actions.

C: Well, Robert curled up in the library makes me think of Elijah sitting down under the broom tree in 1 Kings 19, asking that he might die. But through an angel God makes him get up and go on.

D: I thought of the frightened disciples in the boat with Jesus, and also Jesus appearing to the grief-stricken disciples on the road to Emmaus.

B: Interesting, but to me it's Ezekiel 24 that comes to mind, where God tells Ezekiel not to mourn the death of his wife.

A: God's actions are tough to take in that one!

Sometimes we have to work to hear the full symphony of God's actions in Scripture, even God's apparent lack of action in the face of evil and injustice.

E: In contrast, I thought of 2 Corinthians 12:9, where Paul is assured that God's power is made perfect in weakness.

A: Maybe Robert needed to hear that.

Let's stay in the world of Scripture, and explore God's actions there, rather than prematurely returning to Robert and the case. I'm aware of the fact that none of you have mentioned passages dealing with physical healing.

A: We are disciplining ourselves only to include passages about fear and grief, since we identified those human feelings as the heart of the matter.

D: God's actions are harder to understand in some passages than others, but we're not ignoring them.

Can you summarize the actions of God as they are made known to us in the Scriptures we've identified?

D: Walking toward, joining and teaching the frightened and the sad (in the boat, on the Emmaus road), showing his risen self in the Scripture and sacrament (the Emmaus road), talking of death in the larger context of his life and mission ("Let the dead bury the dead," "My power is made perfect in weakness"), turning their attention from what is limited to what he gives them (the Emmaus road, Elijah, Jonah). I would summarize God's action this way: God situates death inside the bigger reality of his life.

Step 3: Reflection on Students' Responses to Christ's Ministry

Good work. Now let's make the move from our perception of Christ's ministry, as made known in God's actions, to our participation in Christ's ministry. Remember, making this move is no slam dunk! And remember, too, to speak for yourselves and not the participants in the case. In this step you're invited to reflect on your own lives and faith even while remaining compassionate toward Robert.

B: In step two we affirmed that God always sets death in the larger reality of his life. But it's one thing to know that in my head and another to know it when someone is dying or things are falling apart.

All: Our faith needs support and encouragement, even though we are seminary students! We're all like Robert at times.

Return to the story of disciples on the road to Emmaus, and use it to look at your need for encouragement.

C: We, like the disciples, get caught up in loss and become blind to anything else. I like the way Christ responds to the disciples: he listens, chides them briefly, but then moves beyond the limited conversation they're having into teaching them about himself as the risen one in Scripture. Finally, he breaks bread with them.

I know you want to get back to poor Robert. But when you focus on your own various responses, you learn more about human nature, its fragility and resilience.

Step Four: Participation in Christ's Ministry through the Ministry of the Church

We've reached the final step in our reflection process. Now you can step out of Scripture, so to speak, and back into the case and the ministry of the church. Let's look again at the case's last paragraph, that difficult meeting between Robert and the supervisor.

A: Given our previous reflection on God's action, I think we can all agree that the supervisor's expression of disappointment in Robert, on its own, is not a sufficient response, nor is it participating in Christ's ministry, as we've described it.

B: Given what we concluded about the Emmaus Road story, I think the supervisor should invite Robert for coffee, take time to hear about his uncle and his worries, and then talk about God's response to death and loss as the supervisor understands it as described in Scripture and church tradition. They could talk together about what it means to live as a Christian leader at tough times. Eventually Robert might even be able to talk about how he could respond pastorally to other persons similarly caught in the clutch of loss.

C: I'd previously said that Robert's behavior in the library between the services was the key moment. I still think it was. But now I see his decision to withdraw a little differently. Now I see that he is rejecting two forms of Christ's ministry for him—prayer, and the community of the church.

A: In step two we had focused on our own need to be built up in faith, so I think we should re-cast Robert's decision to withdraw in light of that. Christian leaders have to function during worship, whether they feel like it or not. But merely being told to suck it up, be professional, and do your job isn't what Christ says to his own leaders.

All: Right. We deserve more than that simplistic message. We need help in learning what it means to be Christian leaders who can do our jobs when our lives are hard. This is a part of our witness to Christ setting death in the larger context of his life.

QUESTIONS FOR DISCUSSION

1. How might a reflection unfold if you were to create a dialogue between Robert from Click's reflection and the group of students from Brownlee's?

2. If your theology were liberal or liberationist rather than post-liberal, how might it change the way you did theological reflection?

BIBLIOGRAPHY

Killen, Patricia O'Connell. "Midrange Reflection: The Underlying Practice of Wabash Center Worships, Colloquies, and Consultations." *Teaching Theology & Religion* 10.3 (2007) 143–49.

Killen, Patricia O'Connell, and John de Beer. *The Art of Theological Reflection*. New York: Crossroad, 1994.

Lindbeck, George. *The Nature of Doctrine: Religion and Theology in a Postliberal Age*. 25th Anniversary Edition. Louisville: Westminster John Knox, 2009.

Purves, Andrew. *Reconstructing Pastoral Theology: A Christological Foundation*. Louisville: John Knox, 2004.

5

Calm in the Midst of Chaos

Kimberly Clayton, Carol Kuzmochka, and Lorraine Ste-Marie

INTRODUCTION

Clayton:

THE THEOLOGICAL REFLECTION METHOD I use is drawn largely from *The Art of Theological Reflection* by Patricia O'Connell Killen and John de Beer.[1] After *entering the experience* and describing feelings and images that emerged, the reflector identifies *the heart of the matter* in this experience. Once the heart of the matter is named, the reflector begins to search for *insight*, gleaned from scripture, theological and church tradition, culture, and experience. She or he explores such questions as: What factors influenced this event positively or negatively? How might social, economic, cultural, historical, and psychological considerations shed additional light on the event? What in the event was challenging, stimulating, or disturbing? What values informed reflection? How did the event challenge or confirm personal knowledge, convictions about the Christian life, and pastoral leadership? The conversation is broadened by searching for insights gleaned from Scripture and theological and church tradition. The reflector asks what bib-

---

1. Killen and de Beer, *The Art of Theological Reflection*.

lical stories, images, or passages the event brings to mind and what makes the event theological. Where and how is God present in the situation?

Insight leads, finally, to *action*. Killen and De Beer's method of theological reflection seeks to move one out of *certitude* and *self-assurance* (both can prevent growth and new insights and new actions) and into a spirit of *exploration*, where new insights and ways of acting can emerge. At our seminary, there is a strong emphasis on helping students become "imaginative, resilient leaders for God's changing world"[2]; therefore, a spirit of exploration is essential if we are to be transformed and become transformational leaders in the church and in the world. The reflector asks: What have I learned about myself? about ministry and pastoral leadership? about God? What changes are in order, or what new skills do I need to develop?

I present my reflection in the form of an autobiographical reflection by the student intern who brought the case.

Lorraine Ste-Marie and Carol Kuzmochka effectively reveal how to broaden reflection on the heart of the matter in their Asserting section. In this section, additional voices are introduced pushing beyond the student's own insight and perspective. Biblical passages are interpreted, reminding us that God is in control, even in chaos, offering the gift of peace in even out-of-control moments. This central theological claim helpfully reminds us of our limits and God's overarching grace. They delve more deeply still into the heart of the matter, taking seriously the student's concern for "authenticity" by including Martin Heidegger's work.

Ste-Marie and Kuzmochka:

Our method combines key elements from James and Evelyn Whitehead, Patricia O'Connell Killen and John de Beer, and Richard Osmer. We have found that combining these elements promotes depth in both analysis and hermeneutical discourse. The Whiteheads identify experience, tradition, and culture as theological sources. Their method inspires for us a critical awareness of "the influence of the Christian tradition, culture and personal experience on pastoral decision-making."[3] From Killen and de Beer we borrow an "exploration approach"[4] that intentionally situates the reflector

---

2. This is Columbia Theological Seminary's tag line. See *ctsnet.edu*.

3. Whitehead and Whitehead, *Method in Ministry*, xiii.

4. Killen and de Beer, *The Art of Theological Reflection*, 16–19.

at the juncture where experience and tradition interface. We use Richard Osmer for questions to guide the process at each of its steps.[5]

We follow the Whiteheads' three movements of *attending, asserting* and *deciding*. In the first, we attend to cultural and theological themes in particular. The asserting movement "opens a space for listening to various interpretations and insights.[6] The reflector adopts the stance of an explorer[7] who is open to insight gained from wisdom sources in the Christian tradition and who remains sensitive to many different understandings without fear of asserting a particular interpretation. Finally, the decision movement builds upon the best insights of the assertion stage. The Whiteheads emphasized that while sometimes courageous action may follow from the asserting movement, theological reflection often leads deeper into the mystery that both joy and loss may bring.[8]

The Whiteheads assumed a community gathered for theological reflection around a shared problem or issue. We have therefore presented our reflection in the form of a group's collective response to the student bringing the case, thus modeling the way the Whiteheads would have had a group work on a case.

Clayton's process was clearly well designed for a learning cohort because it highlights the central place that others' input plays in deepening insight and expanding understanding. Her questions move reflectors to honor the many interpretations and meanings that might be given to the same event. They help students develop the habit of asking similar questions, become more aware of the limits of their own interpretations, and realize the rich learning that can be generated by considering new perspectives offered by others.

THE CASE

As a pastoral intern in the Anglican Church I was assigned to an urban parish with a pastor who was new to the community. Since he had not presided at an Ash Wednesday liturgy for this congregation he had asked how the liturgy had been conducted in the past, and how many people usually attended. Advised that no more than twenty people could be expected, we

---

5. Osmer, *Practical Theology*, 4.

6. Whitehead and Whitehead, *Method in Ministry*, 5.

7. Killen and de Beer, *The Art of Theological Reflection*, 16–18.

8. Whitehead and Whitehead, *Method in Ministry*, 16–17.

decided to keep the celebration intimate, inviting everyone into the sanctuary[9] rather than having a small number spread out in the nave.

As people arrived we directed them into the sanctuary. This church is not wheelchair accessible, and a parishioner came in earnest to inform us that a woman with a foot injury was outside unable to enter the building. The pastor and I immediately went outside to help her up the stairs. The process took some time, and when the woman was safely seated it was five minutes past the time to begin. Much to our surprise, when we re-entered the sanctuary it had filled with people. There were now about forty people inhabiting a space not large enough for more than twenty five. Realizing we needed to change plans, the pastor invited the people to move into the nave where there was adequate room. As they were moving he realized he had misplaced his homily in the rush to help the woman into the church. We began looking for it frantically. Parishioners caught on that something was amiss. The pastor invited them to help in the search. Finally, a parishioner found it in one of the pews where the pastor had deposited it on his way to offer assistance.

With a good natured laugh, the pastor began the celebration. When a parish leader approached the pulpit to welcome the people, we realized that we had not turned on the sound system. People began to signal that they could not hear. I rushed to activate the sound system only to return to find that the pastor did not have his portable microphone. I hurried to find it. As the pastor was moving toward the people to engage them in dialogue during his homily, the microphone detached from his lapel and the wire became wrapped around his legs. After untangling himself, the pastor made a few good natured comments to which the congregation responded with warm laughter.

Following the celebration, many people warmly greeted us. In fact many of them told the pastor that this was one of the best Ash Wednesday services they had ever attended.

9. In the Anglican tradition, the term 'sanctuary' is used to define the area in the front of the worship space that houses the altar table, pulpit, and a place for the presider and assistants (and may include seating for a choir).

REFLECTION

Kimberly Clayton

Entering the Experience

Many emotions attended my experience of the chaos of this service. Even before the chaos arose, I had been already nervous, never having officiated at an Ash Wednesday service. The act of coming face-to-face with persons, administering ashes to their foreheads, and saying to them "Remember that you are dust; and to dust you shall return" is a highly intimate pastoral act, yet also an awkward and audacious one. I'd gotten to know people in the congregation during my internship, but I didn't have long-term relationships with them. I wanted to sound pastoral, not nervous. I was also nervous because I was still getting to know the new pastor and his worship style. I didn't want to disappoint him by messing up my parts in the service.

During the service however, as one thing after another started going wrong, and I saw the pastor handle the chaos so well, I calmed down and even joined in the humor of it all. The congregation seemed okay with it. To this day, I can still laugh about all that went wrong.

Identifying the Heart of the Matter

Nevertheless, serious questions still linger for me about pastoral leadership amidst chaos. *The 'heart of the matter' for me is how pastoral leadership in worship enhances or diminishes the worship experience for others.*

Searching for Insight

Pastoral leadership can enhance others' experience of worship if the pastor handles chaotic events well. At first, the pastor and I were frantically trying to find his sermon notes. When others began helping us search and the sermon was found, the pastor was able to convey the feeling that we were all in this together. Worshippers were brought together in the non-worshipful act of helping us out of this scrape. His laughter seemed to put everyone at ease. That calm and good-natured way of handling the early mishaps helped the congregation join in laughter later, when he got all tangled up in the microphone cord.

The experience helped me balance my own preference for formal liturgy and perfection in services. My home parish holds a high standard for worship that is solemn in its grandeur and seamless in its execution. They value solemnity and order as ways of honoring God, and those values have shaped me profoundly. If this Ash Wednesday service had occurred at my home church, the pastor would have been upset, the Worship Committee would have been embarrassed, and the congregation would have been uncomfortable, none of which would have enhanced the worship experience. I can now see how a pastor's 'non-anxious presence' and leadership in the midst of chaos helps others to feel calm and continue to participate with open hearts.

Still, pastoral leadership doesn't just happen during worship itself but also in how prepared a pastor is beforehand. This worship event was influenced by a lack of preparedness. The space for it was inadequate. Admittedly, the pastor had tried to prepare well by asking how many people usually attended Ash Wednesday services, and his estimate was just off. (More people attended this year than last, maybe because they were curious about the new pastor. Maybe the weather was better this year. Maybe there was more publicity for the service than in previous years.) But shouldn't leaders always expect more people—not fewer—so that we aren't left like the disciples of Jesus with five loaves and two fish for a crowd of 5,000?!

The lack of preparedness diminished people's worship experience at two points: first, when the parishioner came to tell us that someone could not get into our building; and second, when the sound system had not been turned on prior to the service. In retrospect, I wonder why the parishioners at this church do not take more initiative there. Have they not been empowered to handle such situations? Why did the parishioner come to the *clergy* about the woman needing help? When the clergy jumped in to help, it caused the pastor to misplace his sermon and the service to start late. Why didn't the ushers handle this need? Why isn't there a Worship Committee that attends to details like training ushers and turning on the sound system? If liturgy is truly the work of the people, not just the pastors, then surely other aspects of worship also ought to be shared.

When lack of preparedness becomes a systemic problem, people's ability to roll with occasional chaos in worship diminishes. Although I expressed appreciation above for the pastor's non-anxious presence, I do suspect that people would not find chaos as humorous, or even endearing, if such mishaps occurred often. When the pastor is chronically unprepared, people may think he is careless.

Context does matter. This parish is in an urban setting where the chaos of the streets often crosses the threshold, impacting the church's life. There is more tolerance of interruptions and unexpected happenings. This parish takes a more casual approach to life in general and worship in particular. The leadership does not often have time to get bogged down in frustration when chaos invades, needing instead to react quickly to solve problems as they arise. The ability to solve problems quickly can prevent the worship experience from being diminished.

Finally, it is worth noting the particular service in which all of this happened. The Ash Wednesday liturgy is a solemn service intended to lead worshippers into the Lenten season. It is a time to reflect on mortality and confess sin. Our service was neither solemn nor reflective! In one respect, to have careful plans go awry is fitting evidence of our mortality, our frailty, and penchant for human failure. Even our best efforts are turned to dust! One could analyze this service, then, by saying that when our failings were met with mercy and grace and gentle laughter, all worshippers received a glimpse of God's own gracious response toward the mess we humans can make of things. A different analysis of this service leads to a different conclusion. All the chaos, and the humor it evoked, may have altered negatively the service we had planned. I wonder how the chaos impacted "Nancy," for instance. She is going through chemotherapy treatments and is quite ill. When she came forward to receive the ashes, she looked so frail, even afraid. She may have needed the quiet setting we had intended that night.

Broadening the Conversation

Two potentially conflicting passages of Scripture come to mind. The call of Isaiah (6:1–8) highlights the awesome, holy presence of God in the temple—and Isaiah's reaction that he is not worthy of such a high calling. As pastors, we have a great responsibility to honor God through worship. On the other hand, in Mark 10:13–16, when Jesus' disciples scolded people for bringing children to him because they would be an "interruption," Jesus welcomed the "interruptions," reminding us that the kingdom of God does not value order over inclusion of God's beloved. Pastoral leadership in worship should never become so bound to order as to make no room for spontaneity and 'disorder'! I am still wrestling with the right balance between the competing values in these two passages.

This experience also raised for me the theological theme of Christian hospitality. A woman came to the church unable to enter the worship space. I wonder why the parish has not addressed the issue of accessibility, which is not only a moral necessity but a theological one as well. The Old Testament and the New Testament have countless stories of hospitality to strangers and laws about providing for the needs of others. This parish has a lot of physical plant needs to address, from roof leaks to new paint in classrooms and new computers, and they might wonder where they will find money for an elevator or a wheelchair ramp. But they have to sort through expenses and set priorities in ways that are faithful. In the meantime, they have to find ways to offer access and welcome with dignity to those who come for worship.

Action Moving Forward

I have learned since Ash Wednesday how much I value worship that is well-planned yet I am also learning the value of worship that makes room for the unexpected. I have now learned that a worship service can be well-led not only through grandeur, as in my home parish, but also through chaos. God is present whenever we gather, and the Spirit still speaks even if our microphones don't work! I will need to continue to work on my ability to be flexible and calm in leadership situations especially when things don't go as planned. I would like to be able occasionally to pray the anecdotal prayer someone once told me about: "Please, Lord, let something happen today that isn't printed in the bulletin."

At the same time, my concern for hospitality motivates me to learn more about this parish's accessibility plans. I have an appointment with the Chair of the Buildings and Grounds Committee next week to learn more. I hope I will be able to lead an adult study on Christian hospitality. My hope would be that new ideas would emerge among us that will help break down barriers preventing full participation here—not only physical barriers, but also spiritual barriers to worship as well.

Carol Kuzmochka and Lorraine Ste-Marie

Attending

We hear you expressing a growing awareness that your intense anxiety about miscues, missteps or mishaps during liturgical worship is becoming a hindrance to your effective pastoral leadership. You are consumed with being a good collaborative partner with your pastor and other congregational leaders while still ensuring that things are done correctly during liturgical worship. The experience you chose for theological reflection with our group reveals this tension: you have a desire to be authentic in liturgical leadership and you also perceive a demand for liturgical correctness. On the surface, the case you presented could be read as a simple description of a series of mishaps. However, as you unpacked the case, the real issue that surfaced was your quest for authenticity as you sought to offer the best possible leadership for the faith community. It became obvious to us that this experience was an ideal choice for you to bring to us for theological reflection. Signs of providence and grace are evident to us in your choice.

We would identify several dynamics at work here. You've been shaped by a culture that places great emphasis on the role of the presider to ensure that everything unfolds correctly during liturgical worship. The culture you're steeped in gives priority to correct public performance of liturgical tasks. But now you have a growing sense that being overly concerned about proper performance is interfering with your authenticity.

The miscues throughout the service provided space for your focus to shift away from correct performance. When you observed that many of the participants expressed appreciation for the experience as they left the church that evening, it underlined the fact that the significance of any situation is shaped by our very actions.[10] As you noted, if the pastor had become flustered or demonstrated anxiety, the worshipping community would have most likely become impatient and considered him incompetent. His calm and natural leadership style enabled the community to enter into the experience with the same grace that allowed him to preside over a meaningful prayer service despite the many mishaps. This was a vital source of learning for our entire reflection group.

Theological themes emerge as we look for these qualities within your own pastoral leadership. We wonder if concern for doing things correctly

10. Charles Guindon, "Authenticity and Integrity: A Heideggerian Perspective," in Young-Eisdendrath and Miller, eds., *Mature Spirituality*, 67.

may be excessive if it renders you feeling inauthentic in your partnership with the community, and anxious about mistakes. Can you sense a call to a deeper trust in God's power at work when the community gathers to worship and pray? We can identify two theological themes: trust that partnership with the community is a secure foundation for effective pastoral leadership; and faith in God's power to calm the storms of chaos when mistakes do occur. We identify two scripture passages—Romans 8:28 and Mark 4:35–41—as wisdom sources for these themes. The first scripture passage expresses trust that for all who are called to God's purpose, things unfold for the good. The second passage presents Jesus calming the stormy wind and sea with the command "Peace Be Still!" (Mark 4:39) and reproving his disciples for their fear and lack of faith.

As we explore the question, "What is the pastoral issue or question that contains the most energy for you?" we all agree upon the following: *Authentic pastoral leadership depends upon partnership with the community and trust in God's power working in the whole community. Anxiety about correct performance can render worship leadership superficial.*

Asserting

Our conversation leads us to several assertions. To begin, we would ask you the following question: Do you think you might be behaving like the anxious disciples? We recall Daniel Harrington's study of Mark 4:39. Harrington considers Jesus sleeping in the midst of a raging storm as the ultimate sign of Jesus' utter confidence in God.[11] This helps us all to see that Jesus' command "Peace, be still!" is not only directed to the storm, but is also intended to still the chaos raging within the disciples. Jesus models the calm and confidence that is possible when one knows that trust is in God. This mirrors the confidence and trust with which the pastoral leader is invited to engage any chaos that arises during worship or in other pastoral situations. For you, faith can prevent your desire for anxious control in liturgical leadership from compromising your authenticity and from hindering your trust in God as present and at work in all who participate.

We also remember Joseph Fitzmyer's interpretation of Romans 8: "God's plan and purpose are what is really behind all that happens to

---

11. Daniel Harrington, SJ, "The Gospel of Mark," in Brown, Fitzmyer, and Murphy, eds., *Jerome Biblical Commentary*, 606.

Christians, for he is really in control."[12] That's a direct challenge to the illusion that effective leadership is about the performance of the presider. This leads us to consider the partnership among God, the whole community and the presider. In response to the challenge you brought in this particular case, we encourage you to relinquish anxious control during liturgical worship and to allow God to work in both you and the community. Your presiding pastor modeled this behavior for you.

You have admitted to your need for anxious control. The question of anxious control prompts one of us to offer a philosophical perspective on authenticity. Heidegger says that it is "only in becoming authentic, that is, in striving to take ownership of our own lives that we can begin to achieve the focused and integrated way of living."[13] Your anxiety threatens to make your leadership merely an instrumental practice, not an integrated part of who you are.

We see a connection between liturgy and leadership, reminding us all that Leitourgia, the Greek word for liturgy, means the work of the people. The leader's role is to stand purposefully *with* the community, to facilitate the prayer of the whole community as *one of us*, and to see that the liturgy is celebrated properly. That does not mean anything goes, but it puts leadership into the right perspective.[14] The pastor in your case demonstrated that a proper celebration is best served by a style that is genuine and non-defensive.[15] We have all been brought to a deeper understanding of the Whiteheads' notion that religious authenticity frees people from the "tyranny of the ideal"—the "fears and fantasies around authority" that keep the community dependent on the presider's right performance.[16]

Deciding

Looking ahead, our reflection leads us to encourage you to hear the call to integrity, to recognize your need to focus on authentic partnership with the community, and to let go of the desire to try to control the liturgical worship. Realize that in your supervisor you have a model of effective

---

12. Joseph Fitzmyer, SJ, "The Letter to the Romans," in Brown, Fitzmyer, and Murphy, eds., *The New Jerome Biblical Commentary*, 855.

13. Guindon, "Authenticity and Integrity," 73.

14. Whitehead and Whitehead, *Method in Ministry*, 136.

15. Whitehead and Whitehead, *Promise of Partnership*, 82.

16. Ibid.

leadership, and resolve to continue to explore this pastoral concern with your supervisor's help.

QUESTION FOR DISCUSSION

1. Can you imagine a method of theological reflection that would put the student in Clayton's reflection in direct dialogue with the group in Kuzmochka and Ste-Marie's reflection?

BIBLIOGRAPHY

Brown, Raymond E., Joseph A. Fitzmyer, and Roland E. Murphy, eds. *The New Jerome Biblical Commentary*. Englewood Cliffs, NJ: Prentice Hall, 1990.

"Columbia Theological Seminary." *Columbia Theological Seminary*. http://www.ctsnet.edu

Killen, Patricia O'Connell, and John de Beer. *The Art of Theological Reflection*. New York: Crossroad, 1994.

Osmer, Richard R. *Practical Theology: An Introduction*. Grand Rapids: Eerdmans, 2008.

Whitehead, James D., and Evelyn Eaton Whitehead. *Method in Ministry: Theological Reflection and Christian Ministry*. Rev. ed. Lanham, MD: Sheed & Ward, 1995.

———. *The Promise of Partnership*. San Francisco: HarperSanFrancisco, 1991.

Young-Eisdendrath, Polly, and Melvin E. Miller, eds. *The Psychology of Mature Spirituality: Integrity, Wisdom, Transcendence*. London: Routledge, 2000.

6

The Book Study at High River

Deborah Kerr Davis and Kathleen Russell

INTRODUCTION

Russell:

IN FIELD EDUCATION WE ask students to be storytellers. Tell us a story, we say, about an experience you have had. Capture an event or an incident or a situation in words so that others—a supervisor, a class, a peer group—can explore it, think about it, make meaning of it, and learn something for the future. And students do. Their stories, once told, no longer belong just to the students but also to the listeners, to a community of faith. The story is less a scientific object of study than a glimpse into the mystery of the sacred, less a possession than something held in trust, a gift.

So how do we handle this gift? A narrative approach best honors the form of the student's work and also invites a special kind of relationship—not just with the story itself, but also with the experience and the person behind the story. This is because stories are at the same time revelatory and connective. Using a narrative approach allows the story listeners (or readers) to slow down the meaning-making process[1] and to stay grounded in the particulars. They cannot skip over the messy particulars of human

---

1. Killen, "Midrange Reflection."

life and ministry in a rush to analysis or judgment and they cannot default to problem-solving or advising. A narrative approach works against glibness in sacred matters, against generalizing (so often a form of projection), and a rush to judgment. It invites imagination and playfulness. These are theological commitments in themselves, emerging from my own theology of incarnation and sacramental sense of creation.[2]

Most narratives written in field education are not elaborate literary masterpieces but more like snapshots (to use visual metaphors). They usually represent attempts to capture moments in time, not complete narrative arcs. Keeping this in mind helps the reflector stay in and with the moment depicted. The time for venturing farther afield—say, by constructing counter-narratives or linking to conceptual frameworks—can come later. The immediate challenge is to stay with the narrative at hand, even as it evokes feelings, reactions, and perceptions in the reflector.

This particular case is a story that, while brief, is a complete story. Following a narrative approach, I examine the case's characters, setting, plot, images/motifs/symbols, and, finally, themes, in order to arrive at some conclusions about the nature of the ministerial vocation and its challenges.

Davis:

This case can be assessed through the cutting-edge work of Deborah Hunsinger and Theresa Latini on compassionate communication, outlined in their book *Transforming Church Conflict*.[3] Hunsinger and Latini use as their foundation Karl Barth's theology of human relationships. Barth called the basic form of humanity "being-in-encounter."[4] He meant that we find our humanity as we live in relationship with others. Hunsinger and Latini say that "being-in-encounter" with one another, according to Barth, consists of four things: "mutual seeing, hearing, speaking, and assisting one another with gladness." "Mutual seeing" means looking one another in the eye and

---

2. When practiced in a group, a narrative approach invites those who hear the story to develop habits of observation, deep listening and reflection that can contribute to ministerial formation and practice. This includes the student storyteller who now listens to her own story. Thus the reflection process is about relationship, with the story, and through the story with the experiences of men and women and the movement of the Spirit.

3. Hunsinger and Latini, *Transforming Church Conflict*.

4. Ibid., 15.

seeing the other as well as consenting to being seen.[5] "Mutual speaking and hearing" means that "in order to be known by others, we must risk revealing who we are by speaking to them. In addition, we must listen with care to their own self-revelation."[6] "Mutual assistance" refers to the reality that "no human being is self-sufficient. All human beings need the assistance of others from cradle to grave."[7] Finally, "assisting one another with gladness" is at the core of relationships that respect one another and glorify God, according to Barth.[8]

Hunsinger and Latini correlate Barth's four actions with their own four basic skills of compassionate communication: "observing without evaluating, stating feelings vulnerably and openly, connecting feelings to underlying needs, and making clear requests. These four skills provide concrete guidance for us as we seek to live in this kind of encounter."[9] These categories provide a theological basis for assessing the interactions in this case.

THE CASE

Context

High River is a rural church of about 100 members. At this church there is a monthly book study group which is composed of about ten retired women, aged 60–87. The job description of the field education student at High River is to offer pastoral care to shut-ins, to assist in worship, and preach once a semester.

The Event

About 10:00 p.m. on Sunday night I received a call from Freda, the leader of the Women's Bible Study group, on my cell phone. She began by telling me how good my sermon had been that morning, and then asked me if I have classes on Mondays. I said that Monday I didn't have any classes and I used that time to focus on my family. Freda said she was really happy that

5. Ibid., 15.
6. Ibid., 16.
7. Ibid.
8. Ibid., 17.
9. Ibid., 15.

I was "free" on Mondays because her group was going to read the fictional book based on a story in Afghanistan that I had mentioned in my sermon, and they wanted me to be the discussion leader. She told me that the book group would be at Madge's house the following Monday and then asked if these arrangements were okay. Feeling like I had been given no opportunity to decline the "invitation," I agreed to lead the book study. I was angry when I hung up the telephone because she had called me late at night on my cell phone, because she did not respect my time with my family, and because I felt manipulated into saying yes to something I did not want to do.

Begrudgingly, I prepared for the book study. I reviewed the book, read some critical reviews of it online, and prepared a discussion outline. When I arrived at Madge's house on the appointed day, I was graciously welcomed as the 'honored' guest. After polite introductions, Freda asked me to begin. I began by describing the reason this book on Afghanistan was an interesting book to me, but was quickly interrupted by Madge who said she did not know why anyone would find this book interesting. She had read the first ten pages and was disgusted with the book because it showed how poorly women in Afghanistan are treated, so she refused to read further. A few other people echoed their discontent with the book choice.

I listened and then spoke about how much I like books that have both strong interpersonal relationships and theological themes. We went on with our discussion of the book with me pointing out some of the ways that the main character, a notable man of Afghanistan, had acted heroically. This ignited a conversation about whether someone following another faith can actually be a good and ethical person, the validity of Islam as a path for knowing God, the future of the world if terrorist activities continue and strong words about American patriotism and Jesus.

I tried to discuss how all religions have had factions that have engaged in destructive practices. I pointed to our need to gain knowledge about other religions in order to move to a more global perspective. Someone quickly suggested we adjourn for an early lunch. Everyone smiled nicely and moved on to lunch and small talk.

I left as soon as I could, feeling angry and frustrated. I also left wondering many things. How had I gotten myself into this situation? Could I ever really be a minister in a church where some people have such a narrow way of looking at things? What was being said about me after I left? What kind of report would go back to my supervisor about this chaotic conversation?

Would it impact my chances for success in this placement, given how upset I sensed some of the ladies were with my views?

REFLECTION

Kathleen Russell

The Characters

Who are the people in the High River narrative? Jane, Freda, and Madge are the main characters. They have names, feelings, and opinions. They act, and we hear their voices. But while they are at the center of the story, they are not alone. Hovering around the edges and background of this story are Jane's family, the pastor/supervisor, the rest of the congregation (who also heard the sermon), the rest of the women of the book club, the women of Afghanistan, the "notable" man who acts heroically and even the novel's author. All of these characters are part of the story, but with whom do we start? This story is told from Jane's point of view; she tells her story with honesty and vulnerability. The listener is invited into her world, her feelings, her hopes and disappointments, and her questions more than any of the others. Even though we know something about Freda and Magda from their behavior and comments, our access to their inner lives of faith, feeling and experience is limited. Thus Jane becomes our entrée into this narrative and the focus of reflection.

The Setting

Where does the story take place? As in theater, the setting provides the space within which the drama takes place. Some settings for field education case studies carry a weight of their own. Places like hospital waiting rooms that put people in liminal states, soup kitchens with the busy noises of food being served and people eating, or the way an authority figure arranges chairs in her office all provide a frame that shapes the story. However, in this story, relationship provides the setting for the story. The relationship, rather than a physical space, sets the boundaries and edges to create a defined area within which characters move toward and away from each other. Backdrops may change (from chancel to living room) but the relationship remains the setting for the characters and plot. In Jane's story, the characters act and the story unfolds most intimately within relationships that are defined by the identity and roles of a field education student and lay parishioners. At the same time, as a field education student, Jane also exists in a relationship with her supervisor.

The Plot

What happens? James Hopewell says that plots unfold, thicken, twist and turn.[10] As plots go, this case study has it all. Following the plot line helps the listener attend to the nuances of what is going on with the characters and their relationships. This story's plot unfolds quickly; much happens. It begins when Jane preaches her sermon and ends with her wondering what people are saying about her behind her back. In between, Jane says yes when she wants to say no to leading the book club (a plot twist); her plans for discussing the book evaporate in the face of the book club's resistance to it (an unexpected turn of events); and she is left with deep disappointment as the book club members decamp for lunch (a thickening of the plot).

Images, Motifs, Symbols

The very title of the case is symbolic. "High River," the name the writer has given to the congregation, is suggestive in two ways. First, 'high' is part of a polarity of 'high/low,' bringing to mind something that is over or above something else, an image of separation or distance and possibly hierarchy. However, a high river also evokes a river that is engorged with waters flowing into it from tributaries. A high river has deep waters, a fast current and lots of stuff bumping into each other. Danger lurks. Those who enter a high river might be swept away, caught up in circumstances beyond their control. If the river is at flood stage, it may overflow its banks and encroach on the land.

Themes

A theme serves a unifying function, emerging from and tying together the particulars of the story. Themes involve meaning; therefore, the work of identifying themes in a story gets to the heart of interpretation. So far, the

10. Hopewell, *Stories and Structures*, 153.

narrative approach has followed a built-in discipline of looking at particular elements of the narrative and thus has stayed true to it. Some imagination has been at work (e.g., in asking what the image of a "high river" evokes) but even this was done within a defined framework. However, when it comes to identifying themes in a story the task becomes more subjective: what I see may differ from what others see. Identifying themes thus calls for self-awareness and even tentativeness. The task is one of exploration, trying on, offering, and allowing for multiple possibilities. In a story as rich and thick as Jane's, the thematic possibilities abound, but two seem worth following: those of *disconnection* and *danger*.

DISCONNECTION

Considering all the English words that start with *dis*, its negative meaning as a prefix becomes clear. However, the Latin root *dis* also means *apart, asunder* and *away*—meanings which only reinforce the sense of separation and dissonance that are woven through this story. There is a disconnect between what Jane wants to do and what she does; between what Jane says ("Mondays are for family") and what Freda hears ("Oh, then you are free"); between Jane's hopes for what the book will do for the group and its discipleship and the reality of how the group responds; between being introduced as an "honored" guest and then being "dissed" and dismissed; between the possibilities for Jane's leadership and effectiveness within the book club and her own reactivity; between the situation of the Afghan women in the book and that of the book club members. The 'disconnects' are existential, interpersonal, cultural and theological.

DANGER

Whether she is seduced by praise, possibility, or obligation, Jane steps into a river that ends up tossing her around and threatening her sense of identity and ministry. Jane's vocation bookends this story, starting with the sermon she gives and ending with the doubts and questions she has about her identity ('Are we all Christians?') and her calling to ministry ('Do I really want to do this work?'). In the midst of all this, Jane is tossed about emotionally and bumps into the realities of difficult personalities, cultural bias, and just how hard and how complicated ministry can be. Her own vulnerability to inner conflict and failure put her at risk. Will she get out of the river in order to be safe, or will she stay in and figure out how to navigate the currents of personality and group dynamics and the 'stuff' of expectations, rejection and gaps?

This mix of disconnection and danger reveal something about the nature of the pastoral relationship and ministerial vocation, and it is not a pretty picture. The pastoral relationship is often a double helix of connection and separateness, framed by role and role expectations as much as by needs or desires of individuals. People, both lay and ordained, move close toward one another, but also away, likewise, students and supervisors. Ministerial vocation can and does takes people into surprising, chaotic and unsafe territory, not only in situations and relationships with others, but within one's self. After all, Jesus was baptized in a river, not a lake or pool, in the type of water that can rage and swirl as much as refresh and sustain.

Genre

The dominant themes of danger and disconnection in this story, coupled with the setting of pastoral relationships and vocational preparation, suggest that this is an *initiation story*. It is the story of Jane's emotionally and existentially charged entrance into the hardness and complexity of doing ministry and being a minister. Ira Progoff describes this kind of experience as a "hinge" experience, one that opens the door to something more, something wiser, deeper and more coherent.[11] Of course the door may remain closed; Jane might escape to shore or she might remain in the river barely keeping her head above water, only to emerge downstream battered and exhausted. But if the door remains open, how will Jane move through it? If, indeed, every story intends a future, then what future does *this* story intend? Will it merely cycle through repeated disconnections and dangers, or will it become a story of hope, healing and grace?

Uttering even the very possibility of a hopeful future feels glib, given the pastoral imperative *not* to diminish the difficulty and suffering of a story's characters. And yet, the vocational imperative is to affirm hope, which abides in remembering that this is one story, one experience, in Jane's life. When she meets other Fredas, takes other last-minute calls that challenge her boundaries, and leads other meetings that take her by surprise only to receive other rejections, Jane will be able to act in ways that will make for different stories. The formative experience will thus become transformative.

11. Progoff, *Dynamics of Hope.*

Finally, in sharing her story with honesty and vulnerability, Jane has shared a gift, something entrusted to her, with her peers and teachers. Therein lays perhaps the greatest grace of all to come out of High Water.

Deborah Kerr Davis

The Phone Call

Freda has a job that she wants to get done. She wants someone to lead her book group discussion and zeroes in on the seminarian as her target candidate. Freda then employs the strategies that have probably worked for her throughout her lifetime. She calls late in the evening (not during working hours) and catches Jane off-guard. Freda compliments Jane on her sermon, in order to make Jane more likely to say yes to her request. Freda confirms Jane's availability before making the request. Finally, Freda twists Jane's attempt to say 'no' into a 'yes.' Freda utilizes her well-honed strategies of launching a surprise attack, lulling her target into feeling safe with her, and then moving in for the kill, disregarding any resistance.

We can analyze Freda's behavior employing Barth's categories for healthy being-in-relationship with one another. As Freda seeks to get a leader for the book discussion group does she "authentically seek to see" who Jane is? No. She sees Jane as a means to an end—more as an *object* than *another*. Does she "listen and hear" what Jane is saying in order to have a dialogue about the book study? No. Freda acts according to her own agenda, disregarding the responses she is given in order to achieve her goal. Is the result "mutual assistance given with gladness"? Certainly not! Jane feels coerced and begrudging as she enters this contract.

Jane also has some profound issues in dealing with this congregant. First of all, she has given out her personal cell number and answered a call late at night. This represents a lack of boundaries, although Jane may have seen it as an attempt to be a good pastor who is always available to her congregants. Perhaps she longed to fulfill Barth's category of living with a spirit of assisting others, and wasn't cognizant of the necessary component of *mutuality*. Secondly, when Jane heard her own words "I don't have any classes on Monday and use that time to focus on my family" re-interpreted as "I'm free on Mondays," she let the misinterpretation stand. Jane was neither being seen nor heard but she lacked the courage to reframe the conversation so that Freda could hear her 'no.' Finally, Jane reacted with anger at the manipulation and yet she did not name her needs or feelings during the conversation.

Had the women in this case used Hunsinger's and Latini's compassionate communication skills, this conversation could have gone much differently. If Freda known about these skills, she could have employed the method of making an observation, expressing her feelings, naming her needs, and then making her request. First of all, seeing Jane as another person (not an object to meet a desire), Freda would have called during working hours. Jane would have been in a professional environment and therefore not compromised by a surprise attack. Secondly, Freda could have said, "I noticed that you mentioned the book that my book group is studying in your sermon. I was delighted to know that we have this book in common. I also need someone to lead the discussion of this complicated book tomorrow. Would you consider doing this?" Jane could have then responded, "I am glad that we have this book in common! I would enjoy discussing it with you, but Monday is the day I spend caring for my family and so I am not available that day. Can you and I set up a time to discuss the book so that you would feel capable of leading the book discussion yourself? Or can I recommend someone else who might be able to help?" This would have met the need for mutual assistance, done with gladness.

The Book Study

The book group members were uncomfortable with the choice of this book, its content, and Jane's attempt to get them to see it in a positive light. Jane came to the meeting without "gladness" and then sought to follow the outline she had developed for the event. When the group expressed their unhappiness with the book, Jane kept moving forward with her agenda. When the group questioned the basic premise of the book, Jane became defensive. Everyone was uncomfortable, and so the discussion was aborted. The book group members and Jane were not able to mutually see, hear and listen to one another. Mutual assistance in understanding this book, difficult issues, and each other was not achieved. And all of it definitely transpired without gladness!

Using Hunsinger's and Latini's compassionate communication skills, this book study could have gone differently. Jane might have begun the book group with the statement, "When I read this book I noticed that it had many complex issues regarding religions, politics, and relationships between men and women. Where would you like to begin as we discuss this book?" If the first response was Madge stating the book was "disgusting" because of the way women were treated in it, and others agreed, Jane could have said, "It sounds like you are feeling really angry about the gender issues in the book. Let's begin our study talking about these issues." Perhaps the discussion would have moved forward about gender inequality in Afghanistan and then to the gender inequality the women in the group had experienced.

If later on the conversation had turned to "whether someone following another faith can actually be a good and ethical person, the validity of Islam as a path for knowing God, and the future of the world if terrorist activities continue," Jane might have summarized what she was hearing at a deeper level. She could have said, "I am noticing that many in our group are worried about the state of the world and the future. Would anyone be willing to name what it is she fears during this turbulent time?" Perhaps the discussion then could have proceeded in the direction of talking about their fears of change, growing older, and becoming less in control, powerless. If the conversation were able to go in this direction, the women's needs to be mutually seen and heard, and to assist one another, might have been met in this encounter.

QUESTION FOR DISCUSSION

1. Russell acknowledges that when students write cases, they are giving a gift of their story to others to reflect on. What are the ethics of receiving and using such a gift?

BIBLIOGRAPHY

Hopewell, James F. *Congregation: Stories and Structures.* Philadelphia: Fortress, 1987.

Hunsinger, Deborah van Deusen, and Theresa Latini. *Transforming Church Conflict: Compassionate Leadership in Action.* Louisville: Westminster John Knox, 2013.

Killen, Patricia O'Connell. "Midrange Reflection: The Underlying Practice of Wabash Center Worships, Colloquies, and Consultations." *Teaching Theology & Religion* 10.3 (2007) 143–49.

Progoff, Ira. *The Dynamics of Hope: Perspectives of Process in Anxiety and Creativity, Imagery and Dreams.* New York: Dialogue House Library, 1985.

7

First Take the Log Out of Your Own Eye

Tom Fuller and Roslyn Wright

INTRODUCTION

Fuller:

THE METHOD OF THEOLOGICAL reflection I employ is a slightly modified version of James and Evelyn Whitehead's model—*Attending, Asserting,* and *Pastoral Response.*[1] My three-stage approach might be described as *Observations, Engagement,* and *Response.* In the observations stage, I briefly summarize the case, note points of contact with my personal experience, and identify what I believe to be the most relevant issues for the practice of ministry. I then move on to engage the issues in light of what is revealed in the Scriptures and in reference to Christian doctrine. With other cases, where possible, I may appropriate insights from other disciplines. Throughout this second movement, I aim to develop a composite portrait of broad truths, principles, and objectives that will inform faithful pastoral practice. These are translated into practical steps in the response. I conclude by acknowledging implications for future ministry practice and personal growth.

---

1. Whitehead and Whitehead, *Method in Ministry,* 13.

I have found this methodology useful for reflection on a wide variety of ministry cases. It was especially useful for reflecting on this case in two counterbalancing respects. The case not only contained points of contact with my own experience but also pointed to the normative backstop of Scripture and doctrine to guard against exceptionalism. Pain, fear, and anxiety can have powerful isolating effects, potentially leading to the perspective that my situation is exceptional. Based on my own experiences of difficulty in caring for others with whom I share similar burdens of grief or loss, I found it all the more necessary to establish these guardrails of normative counsel to give direction (and correction) to the voice of personal experience in my reflections.

There is a palpable visceral dimension to Roslyn's reflection. She, of course, reflected in the first person, whereas I reflected in the third person. A first-person reflection on such an emotionally charged case such as this is bound to elicit greater pathos. This is an obvious strength of her methodology: The *Reaction* phase of her approach ripples across the length of the reflection, giving it a flow and unity that is absent from my reflection. I also appreciate the way in which Roslyn engaged other perspectives dialogically. As she acknowledged the voices of Scripture and tradition speaking into the case, she responded to those voices with a mixture of confession and question that was true to the reactionary pathos. This did not, however, derail Roslyn's ability to articulate a coherent and thoughtful response. Rather, she gave it a tone of faithful resolve, much like the closing verses of a psalm of lament.

Wright:

My model for reflection is based on the Action-Reflection learning cycle developed by educational theorist David A. Kolb.[2] Kolb argued that experiential learning happens in four steps, which are: 1. *Concrete experience*; 2. *Observations and reflections*; 3. *Formation of abstract concepts and generalizations*; 4. *Testing implications of concepts in new situations*. Translating these into steps that reflectors take when preparing a case study, I call them *Action, Reaction, Reflection, Response*.

1. *Action*: Reflectors begin with an event from their experience, something that has challenged or puzzled them. They stop and pay attention

2. Kolb, *Experiential Learning*.

to what has happened. They begin by recording as much detail about the event as possible. For purposes of this reflection, I take the case itself to represent this step.

2. *Reaction*: After giving this initial description of the event, they turn their attention to their reactions. Reactions happen at several levels: emotional, physical, and mental (the first spontaneous thoughts). Spending time on the Reaction phase helps bring to awareness aspects of their experience that were originally unconscious. I find the framework of family systems theory helpful in considering what drives automatic, unconscious behaviors, as the theory recognizes the interplay among the dynamics of family of origin, family of choice, and the church 'family.' The more reflectors can uncover here of these dynamics, the more they will be able to engage in Reflection and Response. Considering their reactions also brings into view what has happened to them since the event, and asks them to be clear about why they want to explore it. By recording their reactions, they gain some distance, which allows for more objective consideration, so that they can move into the next phase.

3. *Reflection*: Now they step back and consider the situation from other perspectives. What is happening in the system? What helps to enlarge their understanding? What do the voices of Scripture, the tradition of the church, culture, and society add to the conversation?

4. *Response*: Now they are able to consider what they have learnt through the preparation of their case and what action they now plan to take as a consequence. Ideally, they finalize their response after working through the case in supervision and after the wisdom of others has helped to bring possibilities into focus.

5. *Title*: One last step is to choose a title for their case. This brings a point of focus when they present their case to a group of other reflectors.

Tom's method of speaking from the third person allows for objective considerations and summary, particularly in the *Observation* phase. His *Engagement* and *Response* flow from this. *Engagement* brought psychological understanding of grief process together with biblical perspectives. The skill here is to not slide into preaching about what Harry will experience from this suffering. I would have found questions useful to prompt alternative views. *Response* identifies practical steps and possibilities for sustaining ministry in this situation and beyond. Tom concludes with some wise reminders about the power of our emotions, both as gift and liability, in our pastoral work.

THE CASE

Context

Harry was recently appointed as interim pastor at Oasis, a church of approximately sixty members, located in the suburbs of Sydney, Australia. He was leading the congregation in a review process prior to starting their search for a permanent pastor. Harry was already familiar with the Oasis congregation, having ministered in the area for thirty years. He knew many of the members, some of whom were former colleagues in ministry. One such member was Mary, who works at the seminary where Harry teaches.

Harry's adult children left the Church in their teenage years; they no longer embrace the Church or the Christian faith. In the months prior to beginning his service at Oasis, Harry's son, Robert, was diagnosed with cancer. He is receiving chemotherapy treatments. The church knew that Harry's family was dealing with cancer before they accepted him as the interim pastor.

The Event

Before worship was to begin on Sunday, Harry was greeting members seated in the sanctuary. He saw Mary, and went over to her. He knew that Mary's husband, Fred, was fighting leukemia.

"How are you going?" Harry asked.

"Oh, so-so," Mary responded. "Fred had a bone marrow biopsy on Thursday, and we are waiting to hear whether or not he continues on the current treatment."

"So what is Plan B?"

Mary answered, "Palliative care."

Harry felt a wave of shock roll over him, and he began to weep. Mary looked surprised at Harry's response. She rose from her seat and gave Harry a hug. "It's alright," Mary said consolingly. "Life is good for us; we are doing well. I won't ask how you are. You don't need that at the moment."

"No, don't," Harry replied. "It's obvious, isn't it?"

"You need to go and get yourself ready to preach," Mary said.

Harry moved off, feeling shaken, and took his seat as the service commenced. His pastoral reflection that day was sharing his personal faith story. It was a difficult task. As Harry shared about the ways in which he had known God in the past, he made no reference to his current struggles: dealing with Robert's illness, or his feelings of failure as a parent to pass on the Christian faith to his children.

Reflecting on the morning's events, Harry asked himself, "How can I care pastorally for Mary when this is so raw for me?" He recalled earlier remarks Mary had made about the difficulty of talking about her husband's condition in her work environment at the seminary. Both students and line managers, wanting to express their care and concern, regularly asked how she and Fred were doing. This caused Mary great emotional anguish, to the extent that she felt it compromised her capacity to work professionally. Harry now appreciated what Mary was saying. Perhaps freely sharing his own struggles is not in the best interest, either for himself or for the church community.

REFLECTION

Tom Fuller

Observations

In this ministry case, Harry is overcome emotionally during a pastoral encounter with a parishioner, Mary, who, like himself, has a family member battling a life-threatening disease. The episode takes place just minutes prior to the start of a worship service, in the sanctuary of Oasis Church, where Harry is serving as interim pastor. Both Harry and Mary work at a local seminary. Harry's son, Robert, is battling cancer; Robert does not embrace the Christian faith. Mary's husband, Fred, is fighting leukemia. Harry was blindsided by his own emotional reaction, which was prompted by Mary's reference to palliative care as the sole remaining option should Fred's current treatment prove ineffective. Harry wants to minister to Mary but finds himself too emotionally compromised to do so.

Typically, a minister's capacity to empathize with another's struggle is a prized commodity. There are, however, those times—even seasons—when the other's cry resonates so closely with our own that such a commodity can feel more like a curse. I have experienced similar emotional conflicts on occasion when ministering to persons struggling with the pain of a failed marriage and divorce. Having firsthand experience with the other's pain and grief, I have felt the impulse all the more to come alongside them as a pastoral presence. In some instances, however, the intersection of our respective wounds has been akin to crossing the wrong two wires in electrical work.

Harry's closing question gives voice to the immediate concern: "How can I care pastorally for Mary when this is so raw for me?" The question, however, can be taken in at least two directions: first, How is it possible for *me* to minister under these circumstances? and second, How can I go about ministering to *Mary* under these circumstances? In the first instance, the focus is placed on Harry and his capacity to function pastorally in such a situation. In the second instance, the focus is on how to minister to Mary. While the issues are largely inseparable, each represents a different approach to Harry's question.

Engagement

Grief is part of the human experience in a world marred by sin's effects. Even the prospect (or anticipation) of loss can create tremendous anxiety. While both Robert and Fred continue to receive treatment for their life-threatening diseases, it is reasonable for Harry and Mary to experience some degree of anticipatory grief. This is neither tantamount to their having resigned themselves to their loved ones' deaths, nor is it mutually exclusive of hope for recovery. The looming prospect of such a loss, however, makes grief a legitimate pastoral concern in this case.

The prophet Isaiah describes God's suffering servant as "a man of sorrows and acquainted with grief" (Isa 53:3). This one who would bear our griefs and carry our sorrows (Isa 53:4) is sufficiently and existentially acquainted with those burdens himself. He is not a trained and professional agent of care but a fellow traveler on the difficult road. His care is the off-spring of deep love and deep suffering. He knows our fear and feels our pain. A vivid portrait of his compassion is given us in John 11, where we find Jesus weeping at the tomb of Lazarus. "He was deeply moved in spirit and was troubled" (John 11:33). On display here is the Son of God struggling with his own emotions: He feels for the bereaved and others; he feels with the bereaved and others; and he feels toward the bereaved and others, including those who second-guess his ways (John 11:37). God's suffering servant, the Son whom he sent, knows firsthand the complexity of emotions, the weight of grief, and the burdensome joy of ministry.

Harry seems to feel that he failed Mary in their encounter because he couldn't "keep it together." An involuntary outpouring of emotions can be an unsettling experience, to be sure. Harry must have felt ambushed by his emotions and fearful that the same might happen again. But is it reasonable to operate by a conventional model of "non-anxious presence" in every ministry situation?[3] Was it problematic for Jesus to express his own emotions as he did at Lazarus' tomb? However unexpected and disconcerting Harry's emotions may have been, they were real. Mary, of all people, could recognize and appreciate that. As ministers, we regularly encourage others to embrace and express their feelings. While Harry seems to regard his emotional reaction as problematic in ministering to Mary, he may do well to reconsider the ministry model that informs that perspective.

Harry's capacity for ministry—to Mary or anyone else—is a gift of God (2 Cor 3:5). At several points in his second letter to the Corinthian church, Paul asserts the necessity of God's grace for faithful ministry. "Afflicted. . ., perplexed. . ., persecuted. . ., struck down," gospel ministry is "a treasure in earthen vessels," with all attendant weaknesses and fragility (2 Cor 4:7–9). Even as he suffers under the affliction of his "thorn in the flesh," Paul is given assurance that God's grace is sufficient to sustain him in the work of ministry (2 Cor 12:7–10). This comfort in his own suffering that comes by faith is the very same by which Harry is made able to comfort others in their afflictions (2 Cor 1:3–5). In the economy of God's kingdom, such weakness is prime opportunity for God's surpassing greatness and strength to be made manifest in bold relief.

The grace of suffering, while not often a welcome gift, is one means by which God carries out the work of sanctification in our lives. Further, it is a means for God's ministry through us to others who are suffering. This is the way of the suffering servant, our Lord Jesus Christ, as well as the prophets before him and many saints since. Harry's difficulties in managing his emotions are not inconsistent with this trajectory, but his perspective on his own grief—and on Mary's—will give significant shape and direction to any future ministry to Mary and her family.

3. The term is attributed to Edwin Friedman. See Friedman, *Generation to Generation*.

Response

Harry is bearing some weighty emotional baggage. He was caught off guard by his feelings in this case. Concerns for ministry aside, Harry would benefit from seeing a counselor as he walks this path with Robert's illness. He needs a place to explore his feelings and to discuss instances like this when his grief and anxiety bubble to the surface. This is especially needful if he is to continue in a leadership role in the church. This could be a vital means of grace in his life for this season and beyond.

A follow-up conversation with Mary is certainly in order. Working together at the seminary as they do, Harry may be inclined to speak with Mary in that setting. I believe, however, that he would do well to meet with her outside of the work environment and in a place where either party is free to express emotions (though, of course, with appropriate safeguards observed). Such a meeting will afford Mary the opportunity to inquire about Harry, as she is quite likely concerned. Harry may feel the need to explain himself and his previous reaction, though Mary probably understands them even better than Harry does. In his capacity as interim pastor, Harry is concerned about ministering to Mary and Fred. Quite frankly, in this relationship, it is more likely that ministry will be given and received equally by both parties.

One must ask: Should Harry continue to serve in this interim pastoral position while teaching full-time at the seminary and bearing the emotional load of his son's illness? That is a matter for prayerful consideration and counsel. If he is to continue, he should take honest account of the demands of his role and actively seek support from the congregation for those ministry tasks which may not require his involvement or which he feels may place him in a compromising position. Harry need not live in fear of his emotions; neither should he live under the tyranny of a ministry model that commends emotional detachment. Most importantly, Harry does not have to do this alone. God's grace, in the form of Christian community (at Oasis, at the seminary, and elsewhere), is available to come alongside him, even as Aaron and Hur supported the arms of Moses when they weakened (Exod 17:8–13).

This case is a vivid reminder that we bring our feelings with us into every pastoral encounter. Attending to those feelings is a standard of good pastoral practice. There are times and circumstances, however, when our feelings may lurk in the proverbial blind spots, not easily visible via our conventional checks. As an implication for future ministry, Harry might consider the value of being in conversation with a peer group. Seasoned and insightful colleagues can often help us to see potential pitfalls before they materialize.

Roslyn Wright

Reaction

I (Harry) am shaken by the power of the primitive response that welled up in me, and I continue to be disturbed by it. The grief was overwhelming. Mary looked so calm, and she moved to comfort me. I have no idea what was happening for her in sharing her news, as I was unable to move beyond its impact on *me*. I wasn't so much distressed for Fred, although I do care about him. I was distressed by being brought face-to-face with the reality of the terminal phase of cancer, to see my unnamed fears for Robert brought abruptly into focus through Fred's situation.

In addition to my own grief, I felt ashamed by my response and by being unable to care for Mary in that instance. I know the difficulties she has had with other people's reactions. Mary has shared with me how she has had to compartmentalize her own reactions. Mary had trusted me with this latest development in her story, and I was unable to hold it with her. I failed her.

With some time and distance from this event I have been able to identify some of the dynamics at work. I had not paid sufficient attention to my own needs, and I was caught off guard by my emotions. There are several factors contributing to the anxiety I expressed. First, I feel the burden of responsibility for steering this community through its congregation review process. Second, I want to be seen as doing my job well in the eyes of former colleagues, now members of Oasis, including Mary. Third, preparing to share my personal faith story that day had left me wondering about God's presence in the midst of my family issues. Finally, my son's chemotherapy has been physically and emotionally draining for us as a family.

In my reaction to Mary I was unable to manage my own anxiety. Using the lens of family systems theory, I can now see that I had not paid attention to my anxiety, to my place in the system, and to the connections between the changes and challenges in my own family dynamics and the dynamics of the congregation going through change. I have underestimated the tensions I was carrying between the two.

Reflection

I have some questions about my role as a leader and pastor going through an emotionally challenging period in my life, and I turn to Scripture here. Is it appropriate that I look to the congregation to support me even as I support them? After all, aren't we brothers and sisters in Christ, called to "bear one another's burdens" (Gal 6:2)? Or is this a case of needing to make sure that I "bear my own load" (Gal 6:5)?

I also acknowledge that I have professional responsibilities, ones that are necessary to and contribute to the good functioning of the congregation. I recognize the dynamic that comes with too much transparency, when sharing a personal situation spreads anxiety into the congregation. As much as they want to care for and support me, they still look to me for leadership. If I am not functioning well, then the loss of confidence is infectious.

In this encounter, I was caught out by my lack of preparation. It is not that I can and should have prepared for the encounter with Mary in particular. But with the vantage of hindsight I can see that I had not given enough attention to my personal response to the realities of cancer. I also had many questions I needed to work through with God about my family and how I carry the reality that my child has turned away from the church. The pastoral reflection I had prepared for that day was limited and incomplete because I was afraid to look at the hard questions of the present.

Am I willing and able to trust God in what is happening? Do I believe that God holds Robert in his care and love, even if Robert has turned his back on God? Can I sit with the sense that God is with me, and those I love, in the midst of our pain and uncertainty? The mantra of my life has been Psalm 16:5: "You, Lord, are all I have, and you give me all I need; my future is in your hands."

The words of Jesus bring a new level of meaning to me: "If any want to become my followers, let them deny themselves and take up their cross and follow me. For those who want to save their life will lose it, and those who lose their life for my sake, and for the sake of the gospel, will save it. For what will it profit them to gain the whole world and forfeit their own life?" (Mark 8:34–36) I cannot hold onto, or "save," my own life, let alone Robert's life, or the life of the congregation. I must lay them down, not try to control, but take up my cross—the things that are my responsibility, that are mine to do.

Response

First, I have to begin with making time for prayer. I will also make time to see my spiritual director to explore my resistance toward bringing God the fears and concerns I have been carrying.

Second, I need to be present and accounted for in my family. At this time, we need to be supporting each other and drawing in others who can support us, too, such as the extended family and community in which we live. I will take time just to be around. This may mean reducing my workload.

Third, I will discuss with the congregation leaders what I am able to do for the review process, and what I need to lay down and allow others to take up. It may be appropriate for the congregation to look to how it can best meet its own pastoral care needs so that I can focus with the review team on the review process.

Finally, I will make time to talk with Mary. I would like to acknowledge my own rawness in the situation that limited my capacity to offer her the care and support she needed.

QUESTIONS FOR DISCUSSION

1. Is there a way to guard against the "slide into preaching" in one's reflection that Wright warns against? What is the difference between theological reflection and preaching?

2. Correspondingly, is there a way to guard against the slide into subjectivity that Fuller implicitly warns against, especially in "first-person reflections on emotionally charged cases"? What is the difference between theological reflection and psalms of lament?

BIBLIOGRAPHY

Friedman, Edwin H. *Generation to Generation: Family Process in Church and Synagogue.* New York: Guilford, 1985.

Kolb, David A. *Experiential Learning: Experience as the Source of Learning and Development.* Engelwood Cliffs, NJ: Prentice Hall, 1984.

Whitehead, James D., and Evelyn Eaton Whitehead. *Method in Ministry: Theological Reflection and Christian Ministry.* Rev. ed. Lanham, MD: Sheed & Ward, 1995.

8

Whose Table?

Matthew Floding and Tara Hornbacker

INTRODUCTION

Floding:

MY APPROACH IS INSPIRED by Richard Osmer's theory-praxis method[1] and David Lonsdale's writing on Ignatian spirituality.[2] Osmer identifies four tasks in theological reflection which are enriched by the Ignatian invitation to explore, imagine, feel and respond wisely. The "descriptive-empirical task" calls for an embodied ministry of presence and priestly listening. It involves gathering information that helps one discern dynamics and patterns within events. The "interpretive task" engages the pastoral imagination in wondering about God's active participation in the church and world. It draws upon theories in the arts and sciences. The "normative task" exercises the combined skills of theological interpretation, ethical reflection and experiences of sound pastoral practice to discern God's will for a situation. The "pragmatic task" invites the response of servant leadership

---

1. Osmer, *Practical Theology.*
2. Lonsdale, *Eyes to See,* 115.

within the context of an event that may still be unfolding. In it one discerns strategies for action with an invitation to after-action reflection.[3]

I developed five questions to guide my reflection:

1. *What do I see?*

2. *Why did this happen?*

3. *How does scripture speak?*

4. *What is at stake theologically?*

5. *How might we respond?*

I conclude with a practice I use with students of praying for persons in the case, thereby offering a reminder that cases always arise from real life.

I have written my reflection as if I were the intern in the case.

Hornbacker:

I use a hybrid approach in my method of theological reflection, blending the work of Jeffrey Mahan, Barbara Troxell, and Carol Allen in *Shared Wisdom*[4] with Peggy Garrison's work on worshipful settings for case studies.[5] In our seminary, presenters bring their cases to the reflection group following a liturgical outline. We reflect theologically within the context of a brief order of worship that includes an Invocation, a Heritage Connection (typically the singing of a hymn), a Contemporary Story (the reading of the case), Focus Questions (reflection on the case), a Blessing, and a Closing Hymn. This method cultivates an increasing awareness that all our work is worship.

Three questions focus the process of theological reflection itself:

1. *What is really going on here?* (WIRGOH)

2. *Where is God in all this?* (WIGIAT)

3. *What is mine to do?* (WIMToD)[6]

Woven into this process is an engagement with different areas of wisdom.

---

3. Osmer, *Practical Theology*, 4.

4. Mahan, Troxell, and Allen, *Shared Wisdom*.

5. Garrison, "A New Case Method," 177–9.

6. Several authors have claimed origin of these three questions, but they are commonly used in field education settings to guide theological reflection, critical analysis, and discernment.

I have presented my reflection in the form of an order of worship, with the reflection on the case itself written in the first person plural to represent the collective voice of a group.

THE CASE

Context

Gloria Dei is a small rural church in the Wesleyan tradition. It is composed almost exclusively of an aging population. Many of the parishioners grew up in this church and have lived in this community their whole lives; others have returned or moved to its peaceful setting for retirement. The church ethos is deeply traditional, although the congregation is working to attract younger members and thus is trying to be open to some contemporary additions to the worship. The current pastor, Pastor Olivia, has been a key catalyst in this effort; she is respectful of the congregation's fairly reserved tastes but also committed to inviting a more diverse demographic. Responding to her lead, the congregation has become authentically warm and welcoming to any visitors who do come, and they are remarkably supportive of those who enter the church needing some sort of help. I am the intern at Gloria Dei, and I have been serving in this field education placement for nearly three months.

Gloria Dei is an organizing center for many of the parishioners' lives. Pastor Olivia, understanding this, has developed a variety of ways for members to connect with each other at church and to encourage each other as disciples of Jesus Christ. She also celebrates their commitments in the community and affirms the leavening effect these have.

The congregation of Gloria Dei has 'adopted' two teenagers, Steven and Danielle, who first became involved with the congregation several years ago when they knocked on the door during a vacation bible school program and asked what they needed to do to eat. These siblings—now seventh and eleventh grades—come from a broken and challenged background. Several from the congregation have taken responsibility for getting them to youth group or other events. Danielle and Steven are inconsistent members of the church's small youth group (which averages six to eight kids, including them) and only rarely participate in Sunday worship services. They have not been baptized or confirmed, nor have they made any profession of faith. However, they have attended youth group for several years now and have a basic grasp of terminology while still struggling with the stories of scripture. Danielle, for instance, asked me if the Last Supper was the thing that happened right before "Jesus killed himself."

Event

Last Sunday was Youth Sunday, a service of Communion planned and led by the youth. For several weeks, Pastor Olivia had talked with the youth group about the symbolism and the meaning of taking Communion, and each of the youth shared some thoughts about it during the service. Steven and Danielle were active participants in the entire service and took on liturgical leadership roles as assigned by Pastor Olivia. They each played a role in a 'mime communion' in which the communion liturgy was acted out in the context of a story. At the end of the mime communion, the siblings were paired to serve at one of three serving stations for the actual Eucharist. Pastor Olivia and I each served with other members of the youth group.

I felt a bit of discomfort over the fact that communion was being served by people who would not necessarily even identify themselves as Christians. But I simply followed the pastor's lead. As interns tend to do, I 'went with it.'

Ultimately, we received overwhelmingly positive feedback from the congregation regarding the Youth Sunday service, including several comments about how reverent it had been. But I remained somewhat discomforted. I had been moved to see Danielle and Steven rise to a respectful dignity through their engagement with the liturgy. But as for their becoming communion servers, questions lingered.

REFLECTION

Matthew Floding

What do I see?

I see Pastor Olivia working hard at helping Gloria Dei become a warmly welcoming community where there is a sense of belonging. Danielle and Steven's story fits into this narrative of welcome and support. They are not burdened with expectations, but space is created for them.

I see Steven and Danielle showing up. Not to church much, but to meaningful participation in youth group when they can. Every time they show up at youth group I feel joy. I see two youth who are navigating truly difficult life challenges but who nevertheless show up of their own initiative! I imagine God's Spirit at work in their lives as they willingly participate in opportunities like this Youth Sunday communion service.

On that particular Sunday, I saw Pastor Olivia practicing liturgical catechesis as she sensitively taught the meaning of the Lord's Supper, and its place in worship, to the youth. I experienced myself trusting the pastor's theological insight and pastoral practice presiding at the Lord's Table. At the same time, when I explore my feelings on that day even further, I acknowledge that I also felt anxious because I found myself disagreeing with her practice. I felt unsure because I have not encountered the situation of having persons neither baptized nor confirmed serving communion before.

Why did this happen?

Gloria Dei is living into its identity of a place of belonging, not just inclusion. Inclusion makes space, belonging makes sacrifices. Several members have made commitments over a number of years now to support Steven and Danielle's spiritual journey by making themselves available so that the pair can participate when they can and when they wish.

Pastor Olivia intended to reinforce the message of creating space for belonging by letting the two siblings fully participate in the youth group's Eucharist service. Her conviction is that by acting out the gospel in the mimed Eucharistic service and by participating in the sacrament—the "Word made visible," as Augustine put it—they are drawn closer by God's grace to Christ himself.[7]

How does scripture speak?

I have to admit that my first thoughts at the time were about Paul's warning in 1 Corinthians 11:27 about eating the bread and drinking the cup in an unworthy manner. Since then, I have discovered that Paul wasn't done with his teaching on the subject of the Lord's Supper and community. Just a few

---

7. St. Augustine, as quoted in Fitzgerald, *Augustine*, 744.

verses later, he says "About the other things, I will give directions when I come" (1 Cor 11:34).

That discovery led me to ask the question, "Whose table is it?" This allowed me to take a step back and affirm that the communion table is, in fact, Christ's table. This in turn took my mind to other tables, and other meals, in the gospels. It seems that Jesus was often being accused of eating with the wrong people. Mark 2, for example, records the calling of Levi and the feast in Levi's home afterwards. The reaction of the scribes to Jesus' eating with this crowd was, "Why does he eat with tax collectors and sinners?" (Mark 2:16). At this table of gratitude, clearly Levi feasted as one who had responded to the call to follow Jesus. Others at the table, like the twelve, were committed to following Jesus, if not yet entirely convinced that Jesus was sent from God with authority to proclaim the good news of the kingdom of God, to teach, and to heal. Surely a number were curious—their nascent faith being nurtured at the table—like Danielle and Steven.

Pastor Olivia seems to have been acting on such an understanding of how Scripture speaks, and exercising pastoral wisdom, when she encouraged the siblings' sense of belonging to the congregation of Gloria Dei and even of belonging to Jesus. Nevertheless, I can't escape the fact that Christ was host at the Lord's Supper.[8] The apostles, including Paul, were charged with celebrating the Lord's Supper. Paul wrote, "I received from the Lord what I also handed on to you" (1 Cor 11:23), indicating that the tradition of the Table with which he had been entrusted he now was passing on to appointed elders. Studying these texts leaves me at odds with Pastor Olivia, while feeling that my uneasiness is grounded in a reasonable reading of Scripture.

What is at stake theologically?

Embracing the mission of God, while adhering to faithful practice at the Table, is at stake in this seemingly small event at Gloria Dei. The congregation has committed itself to a new disposition towards its surrounding community. I am witness to Pastor Olivia's patient pastoral work in guiding them into a new perspective on their mission as participating in *God's* mission. This is nothing short of a paradigm shift for them. We learned about this altered perspective in our evangelism class. We read missional church scholar Darrell Guder, who wrote that "the biblical message is more

8. Matthew 26:26–29.

radical, more inclusive, more transforming than we have allowed it to be. In particular, we have begun to see that the church of Jesus Christ is not the purpose or goal of the gospel, but rather its instrument and witness. . ."[9] There are signs of this shift taking place in the ministry of Gloria Dei, Danielle and Steven's belonging providing evidence.

This shift calls to mind for me the difference between bounded and centered social sets.[10] When it acts like a bounded set, the church is concerned with the distinction between who is in and who is out of the group and often has very clear notions of how one gets in. A centered set church is one that is centripetal, drawing people into the center where Word and sacraments are celebrated and the vision and values of the Kingdom are re-orienting the group's life together. This is too simple an explanation, but Gloria Dei is moving in the direction of becoming this second kind of church, drawing persons like Danielle and Steven into the life of God in Jesus Christ by the Spirit.

This ecclesiological shift is grounded in God's disposition toward us. God is for us. Karl Barth understood the covenant with Israel fulfilled by Jesus Christ to be the will of God fulfilled for our sake, the "loving kindness of God" actualized.[11] If God so commits to us, including our neighbor, as we know God in Jesus Christ, then it follows that participating in God's mission will be marked by covenant loving kindness towards all.

Specifically with reference to the sacrament of Communion, what is at stake is participating in the covenant loving kindness of God in Jesus Christ as directed by Jesus, practiced and preserved by the apostles, and those who received the tradition.[12] Faithful administration of the sacrament does not diminish for Steven and Danielle "that the very powerful and almost entire force of the Sacrament lies in these words: 'which is for you,' 'which is shed for you.'"[13] This is the gospel disposition which Gloria Dei is growing into, one which I must increasingly embrace; and the heart of the message for Danielle and Steven.

9. Guder, *Missional Church*, 4–5.

10. See Hiebert, *Anthropological Reflections*, chap. 6, for discussion of social set theory and mission.

11. Titus 3:4; Barth, *Dogmatics*, 35–39.

12. For example, the Didache records the tradition, "No one is to drink of your Eucharist but those who have been baptized in the name of the Lord. . ." in Radice, *Early Christian Writings*, 232.

13. Calvin, *Institutes of the Christian Religion*, 362.

How might we respond?

On a personal level, I need to own my theological convictions with humility. I'm serving in this field education experience in a tradition that is not my own and it is as important to understand as to be understood. For me this means I need to engage Pastor Olivia collegially and share my convictions respectfully. I need to trust the relationship we've developed because "meaningful reflection on practice also ultimately depends on mutual trust."[14]

Similarly, to participate in God's mission means that Gloria Dei, Pastor Olivia, and I will continue to encounter awkward moments in which the Spirit's work will be too sublime to comprehend fully. This too calls for humility—and expectancy. God is already at work!

Therefore, this opportunity invites me to celebrate where God is already at work in Danielle and Steven's lives, walk alongside, and encourage more spiritual feeding so that God's Spirit, who produces growth, may nurture them extravagantly.

This experience calls Gloria Dei and its pastoral leadership to keep growing and keep actively expressing covenant loving kindness with a disposition of openness towards all so that more Danielles and Stevens can, in a fully faithful way, "taste and see that the Lord is good" (Psalm 34:8).

> *Christ our host,*
> *You satisfy those who come hungry and thirsty to your Table.*
> *May the community of Gloria Dei be so marked by your hospitality that friend and neighbor, like Steven and Danielle, are drawn into your loving kindness known in the breaking of the bread and the sharing of the cup.*
> *We ask this through Jesus Christ the bread of heaven and the vine in which we find life.*
> *Amen.*

14. Blodgett, *Becoming the Pastor You Hope to Be*, 112.

REFLECTION

Tara Hornbacker

Invocation

Holy One, We come to this time, imagining so many ways to be in ministry. Help us see the ways in which you are using us as vehicles of your grace and generosity. May the ways in which we bear witness to your glory show hospitality to a world desperately seeking your face. In the name of Jesus, we pray, Amen.

Heritage Connection

Hymn *I Come With Joy*[15]

Contemporary Story

Whose Table?

Focus Questions

WHAT IS REALLY GOING ON HERE? (WIRGOH?)

What seems really to be going on here is the intern's sense of ongoing discomfort with the two teenagers serving communion. Many of us would feel the same discomfort. We feel it stems from trying to balance the impulse toward hospitality found in many of the scriptures with the specific teaching of 1 Corinthians 11:27 admonishing Christians against taking communion without proper understanding. For the early Christians, the participatory drama of communion is held in varying degrees of esteem by different congregations. The congregation in this case study is characterized as "traditional," suggesting high esteem for communion, but they have also taken in these two young people, a practice of hospitality. So how should the 1 Corinthians passage be interpreted for them? It is common in scriptural interpretation to question which biblical instructions are

15. Wren, *I Come With Joy*.

socio-cultural norms from the setting of the biblical text and which ones are practices to be observed today without accommodations for a different time and place. We would want, then, to question scripture in this regard before drawing any conclusions about what is—and should be—going on.

We note that this case is set in the midst of a worship service for Youth Sunday. Many of our congregations suspend some of their traditional leanings on such days for more openness toward different practices and innovations that the youth may want to introduce. Part of what is going on here might be the congregation's acceptance of variant youth practices.

There is yet another aspect to consider. The wider culture beyond our congregations is shifting, and it makes the traditional ways of bringing people to faith less effective. In the past, many congregations thought about discipleship in this order: believe, behave, and then belong. In other words, in order to become a member of a congregation, first a person should come to belief; then, out of that belief, they will behave. Once a person "behaves like a Christian," then, they are welcomed into fellowship. With the shifts in culture of the last several decades, a different order is emerging: belong, believe and then become. Most people need to *belong* their way into belief so that they can live out the faith, or *become*. This order is arguable, too. Most agree that *belonging* people into the community must come first.

WHERE IS GOD IN ALL THIS? (WIGIAT?)

This case study moves into a discipleship space if we can see a possible teaching moment in the teens serving communion. Perhaps the WIGIAT question has an answer in a table that is multivalent. God can work through this table as a traditional remembrance of the communion of the body of Christ. God might also be at work as the body of Christ welcomes these young people into the loving embrace of a caring community. The table of the Lord has the capacity to create something new here.

If we can look at this case from the standpoint of the table creating space for something new, other scriptures came to mind. Isaiah 43:19 reminds us always to perceive the ways God is "doing a new thing." Or perhaps the youth serving communion is a glimpse of "a New Jerusalem" when everyone would be present, as in Revelation 21:2–5. Processing this case becomes a truly joyous time for us of treasuring the possibilities of how God could be working in this congregation and through its ministry with these young people. Grace and generosity are alive in this congregation!

What Is Mine To Do? (WIMToD?)

Few of us have ever faced this exact situation, but in most of our traditions there is always conversation as to whether children in the congregation should participate in communion, especially in those traditions that practice adult baptism. Many of us have watched congregations move toward a practice of leaving it to the parents to decide about their children's participation in the bread and cup communion.

An even more common conversation in the Church of the Brethren is whether and how children might be included in Love Feast. Love Feast is a celebration of communion that includes feet washing, a simple communal meal, and the bread and cup communion. Traditionally, only baptized members would participate in this service. More recently, Church of the Brethren congregations have used Love Feast as a teaching opportunity, so that while adults are participating in another room, children are being led through a teaching service. They are offered a simple explanation of what the adults are doing. This teaching service model might provide an alternative for other congregations, such as the one in this case.

In conclusion, we affirm the impulse of the intern to question the event and to pray for clear discernment as his ministry unfolds with the congregation and the youth. We are far from feeling fully satisfied with the events and the theological soundness of the worship in this case, and we remind ourselves that generous grace is not cheap grace. But we pray that Gloria Dei will continue to accompany its youth.

Blessing

We are grateful for the wisdom shared in our group today and for the tie that binds us together in Christian love.

We pray a blessing on this congregation of Gloria Dei in their journey of accompaniment. We bless these youth and hope that they will grow into mature Christians, with a clear sense that they belong to Christ through these loving people. We bless the intern and his ministry in this place. Amen.

Concluding Hymn

Blessed Be the Tie that Binds[16]

16. Fawcett, *Blessed Be The Tie That Binds.*

QUESTION FOR DISCUSSION

1. How does your own tradition reflect critically on your own tradition?

BIBLIOGRAPHY

Barth, Karl. *Church Dogmatics* IV/1, *The Doctrine of Reconciliation*. Edinburgh: T. & T. Clark, 1956.

Blodgett, Barbara. *Becoming the Pastor You Hope to Be*. Herndon, VA: Alban, 2011.

Calvin, John. *Institutes of the Christian Religion*. Edited by John T. McNeill, John T. Translated by Ford Lewis Battles. Philadelphia: Westminster, 1977.

Fawcett, John. "Blessed Be the Tie That Binds." 1782; *alt. The New Century Hymnal*. Cleveland: Pilgrim, 1995.

Fitzgerald, Allen, ed. *Augustine through the Ages: An Encyclopedia*. Grand Rapids: Eerdmans, 2009.

Garrison, Peggy L. T. "A New Case Method: Worship as a Model for Case Analysis." *Journal of Supervision and Training in Ministry* 19 (1998) 173–181.

Guder, Darrell L., ed. *Missional Church: A Vision for the Sending of the Church in North America*. Grand Rapids: Eerdmans, 1998.

Hiebert, Paul G. *Anthropological Reflections on Missiological Issues*. Grand Rapids: Baker, 1994.

Lonsdale, David. *Eyes to See, Ears to Hear: An Introduction to Ignatian Spirituality*. Rev. ed. New York: Orbis, 2000.

Mahan, Jeffrey H., Barbara B. Troxell, and Carol J. Allen. *Shared Wisdom: A Guide to Case Study Reflection in Ministry*. Nashville: Abingdon, 1993.

Osmer, Richard R. *Practical Theology: An Introduction*. Grand Rapids: Erdmans, 2008.

Radice, Betty, ed. *Early Christian Writings*. New York: Penguin, 1981.

Wren, Brian. "I Come With Joy." 1968; rev. 1982, 1994. *The New Century Hymnal*. Cleveland: Pilgrim, 1995.

9

The African Connection
Reflecting on a Mission Trip

Isabel Docampo and William Kincaid

INTRODUCTION

Docampo:

I APPLY A FRAMEWORK of identity and God-talk using postcolonial theology and critical analysis. It is extremely important to start with an examination of identity as a way to become self-aware of the imbedded assumptions we hold of God. Often we assume that we must come to our understanding of God objectively, in spite of the shifts theologians are making in theology to take seriously personal stories. I describe the way I examine identity as looking through a 'wide angle lens.' Through the lens we look at how current and historical political, social, religious and economic institutions and movements influence our personal stories. This awakens us to how our thoughts and biases were shaped and why. It gives us the opportunity to consciously accept or disavow these influences. It also reveals how incomplete our identity and perceptions of God are when we see that they are limited by our context. It helps us become aware that someone in our same city but with a different experience of institutions and movements might offer us an alternative perception that enlarges our questions and experiences with God.

In their introduction to *Postcolonial Theologies*, the editors quote New Testament scholar Fernando Segovia who explains postcolonialism as covering both a "temporal (what-follows-the-colonial) as well as a critical application (what-questions-the-colonial)."[1] The editors, therefore, posit that postcolonial analysis "pursues this historical archeology in order to shed light on the aftermath of that imperialism. This aftermath persists. And thus, postcolonialism is a discourse of resistance to any subsequent related projects of dominance—as, for instance, those of economic globalization and United States hyperpower."[2] Postcolonial theology is a theology from people whose voices have not been fully validated and may offer much needed corrective to the assumptions imbedded in a persistent superiority of a Western worldview and its theologies.

But how does postcolonial analysis help church leaders and laity live into our faith with integrity? We are part of a world where technology and globalized economies have given rise to globalized human slavery, misogyny, and the dissolution of indigenous communities. As a result, the Christian Church (along with other world religions) is being redefined across the globe. More than ever, critical theological reflection is needed to bring healing and reconciliation to a globalized world of suffering. I believe that our identity and God-talk are constructed by how we are related to voices from across the globe as well as those marginalized within our own country. These voices are therefore essential as they shape our relationship with God and our faith practices just as much as we shape theirs, even when we are not fully conscious of it. Coming together into full awareness of each other, in a spirit of humility, we move closer to fully experiencing God's transcendent and transformative revelation for globalized healing.

I resonate with Dr. Kincaid's methodology and I applaud his ability to create three questions that are succinct and yet lead to further questions for deep reflection.

1. Keller, Nausner, Rivera, *Postcolonial Theologies*, 6–7.
2. Ibid., 7–8.

Kincaid:

A student of mine named Mike provided a wonderful definition a few years ago of ministerial reflection. Mike said, "It's like I have all these boxes—my personal life, my family, my studies, my ministry setting, and all these others—but the boxes never talk to each other. Seminary is teaching me the importance of the boxes talking with each other."

Mike's image succinctly captures how I approach the task of ministerial reflection. I engage in mutual critical correlation by asking three questions that get "the boxes talking with each other."[3] The process continues by probing the responses for creative possibilities.

In my approach, the first two "boxes" that talk to each other are the **minister and the experience itself.** At the heart of ministerial reflection is a deep, dynamic commitment to be present in and to an experience in ministry and to remain open to the larger questions of faith and ministry. And so, the first question is: 'Have those undergoing the experience entered into it to the degree that they are sufficiently present to the risks of courage and vulnerability?'

The second question involves an exchange between gospel and context, allowing questions like these to emerge: 'What stories, practices and priorities represent Christian faithfulness?' 'How does the gospel bless, affirm, judge or condemn the context(s) named in the case?' 'How do the concrete realities of the lives of the ministers surface biblical and theological themes that are at the heart of the gospel?'

The third question arises at the intersection of resources and strategies: 'What resources can be brought to bear on this situation?' 'What specific strategies will support a ministry that blesses the lives of those ministered to?' 'Are the strategies aimed at the particular challenge or opportunity or are they so general in nature that the status quo is likely to be maintained?'

Once all the questions are on the table, a lively, discerning theological reflection likely follows an unpredictable path back through the boxes, as a strategy raises questions about theology, or consideration of context triggers personal issues for the minister, or an exploration of resources fosters new courage for the work of justice.

Since our case itself tells the story of a group doing ministerial reflection, my reflection takes the form of a critique of their reflection.

---

3. For an extensive theological background on question-based, correlational approaches, see Browning, *Fundamental Practical Theology.*

I appreciate Dr. Docampo's reflection and wish to affirm three parts in particular. First, she clearly situates the work of reflection in community, emphasizing that we are intended for each other and are called to lean toward each other. Second, she articulates the risky nature of theological leadership. And third, she offers a broad and deep analysis of the pervasive systemic factors that can so utterly confound a group and stall its reflection.

THE CASE

Context

The context is a church-sponsored ministry to orphans in Kenya, Africa. Linda, the pastor of a suburban Houston church, leads teams annually to work with the orphanage. Many of the same team members went on the work trips year after year. They are all between the ages of 35–60, white and upper middle class. Linda's experiences in Kenya have shaped her leadership. She has become conscientized to the problems of global poverty. Her theological views have changed, as she has been increasingly reading liberation and postcolonial theologians.

This year, dissatisfied that in the past her participants had lacked any political or economic analysis to complement their charity work, Linda added to her pre-trip education information on the effects of globalized economic and political institutions on Kenya. She also added a question to the team's daily devotional: "How is God calling the Christian church to bear witness in the globalized disparity of wealth and poverty?"

Event

The team completed a new dormitory and spent evenings reading and singing with the children. They were profoundly moved by the poverty and also by how they were repeatedly thanked. They had all read the new pre-education information and said that they welcomed it. The new devotional question, however, was challenging. The first four days it went unanswered. Linda allowed silent reflection.

Linda did overhear some team members raising the question of the church's calling with the orphanage's staff. In response, they learned some of the children's heart-breaking stories and that they picked tea for less than

$.50 a day; and that adults worked for similar wages in fields and/or factories related to western companies.

On day five, Corey ventured a response during the devotional time, saying, "I know Jesus would go into parliaments and board rooms with a whip, like he did with the money changers' tables, to rage against globalized politics and economics creating poverty. But this is too big for us to fight against, even if I know it's wrong!" A spirit of despair, anger, and helplessness pervaded the room. Linda was distraught that the devotional had taken this turn. Thinking of nothing to add, she closed the discussion with silent prayer.

The next day, Sheila began what turned into a lively but heated discussion. Edgily she said, "We are making life better for the children by sharing our resources; that is how God wants us to witness. And I don't feel guilty about our blessings!" Grace responded gently, "I think that is a good answer but it's not complete. Now when I buy tea at discount prices, I will think of my new friend, Ezekiel, picking the leaves." Mark said a staff member explained to him that fair trade gave fairer wages and that he places the children with growers who are participating in fair trade as often as possible. Sheila offered, "The gift of hospitality I received here is calling me to volunteer at the homeless shelter—not just to dish out food, but to build relationships." Jim interrupted Sheila to say, "This question mixes politics, religion, and money; they don't mix!" At first, Jim's interruption silenced the group, but eventually Corey said that this trip has made him see that politics, money, and religion are all mixed up in our lives; and in these children's lives, but not for good. "I feel good about our mission work that has witnessed to God's hope and compassion. But, I can't help wondering, doesn't God want us to use our resources to make globalization work for these orphans and eliminate the need for mission trips?" Eagerly, Linda said, "Yes, Corey's right! These mission trips must change us, change our faith, and make us change the world!"

REFLECTION

Isabel Docampo

What is the core issue for theological exploration?

The mission team in this case study had a transformational Divine encounter that re-framed their individual and collective identity, faith and worldview. The question for theological exploration is: *How does God reveal the Godself in our inter-human relationships and how does this revelation shape our faith practices?*

Identity and God-talk

In this case study the mission team's identity became complicated when it became aware of the postcolonial economic and political realities of the 21st century affecting their African mission partner friends. The postcolonial theology of God framework espoused by Mayra Rivera helps to describe what the mission team experienced:

> One would have to grapple, for example, with the dependence of the First World on the goods produced by the Third World, with the reliance of the U.S. economy on the exploitation of citizens of other countries;. . .We must be mindful of the fact that we arrive at each scene too late: the processes of appropriation and othering have already begun and our encounters are not independent from them.[4]

The case study implies that the previous mission trips had forged friendships of trust between the African orphanage Christian leaders and the church mission team. These friendships made possible candid conversations about the root economic systems that created the orphanage's dependence on church and other non-governmental organizations. When the team experienced the negative impacts of the globalized economy on health, housing, educational opportunities, basic community infrastructure (running water, electricity and roads) in this African village, they began to make connections to similar impacts on marginalized residents of Houston. They began to see how the same Christian humanitarian aid that mitigated the effects of the globalized economy on the lives of the poorest (in Houston or Africa) was, perversely, supporting an unjust economic and socio-political flow of power! They were unwittingly oppressing their African friends with power they did not realize they possessed, and they were discovering how "Identity is always constructed in relation to others. We cannot understand ourselves without listening to others, especially those we have oppressed or have the potential to oppress."[5]

4. Rivera, *Touch of Transcendence*, 108.

5. Pui-lan, *Postcolonial Feminist Theology*, 60.

This shift in worldview also shifted the team's identity and the perceived identity of their African friends. They realized that they interpreted their experiences incompletely by filtering them through a U.S. or Western lens. According to Edward Said, a Western lens is one that sees the self as liberally open to others, resourceful, understanding historical events as objective realities and rationally offering helpful intervention.[6] Implicit within this identity is the perpetuation of a stereotype of the African as weak, closed off, subjectively irrational, lacking resources and needing intervention. Looking at themselves and their African friends through a non-Western or African lens allowed them to see the flaws in their identity. Doing so brought into sharp focus the resourcefulness, faith, hope and creativity (if not ingenuity) of their African friends' faith practices in a context of devastating complex economic, social, and political realities. The team was profoundly touched by the persistent strength and power of their African friends' faith and humbled that God had brought them together.

God became palpably present to both the U.S. mission team and their African friends. By working together and sharing lamentation, confession, and hope in the worship of God, they all saw God's image looking back at them through the eyes of the Other. All grieved with God over the destructive institutions that had shaped their relationship even before they had met. God revealed the Godself more profoundly than in their previous experiences.

Rivera's postcolonial theology of God asserts that we cannot fully see or know ourselves and transcend the realities of our gender, race, socioeconomic and family experiences until we see our reflections in one another. But how do we transcend our realities in relationship with each other? Rivera writes: "Encounters co-constitute who we are. The transcendent Other leaves her trace on our flesh."[7] Or, as Gayatri Chakravorty Spivak puts it, "to be human is to be intended toward the other."[8] Rivera's theological framework of God's irreducible and mysterious nature begins with a womb image of God-Sophia in creation. This image helps us to visualize umbilical cords and placentas that intimately bring together Creator and humanity with its birthright diversity. We are birthed in relation to one

6. Said, *Orientalism*, as cited by Raheb, *Faith*, 28–29.

7. Rivera, *Touch of Transcendence*, 116.

8. Spivak, *Death*, 36, as quoted in Rivera, *Touch of Transcendence*, 123.

another. God is "not just saying, but bringing forth from within Godself . . . in the beginning was touch."[9]

According to such a theology of God, loving our neighbor as ourselves is precisely how we can come to love and fully know ourselves as created in God's image. This theology of God challenges the undercurrents of the U.S. myth of independence that creeps into our God-talk about individual paths for salvation devoid of any need or connection to the Other save to offer charitable acts of compassion. This theology also challenges religious doctrine of absolute truths that create exclusivist practices based on religion, race, ethnicities, gender, class and sexual orientation. The Greatest Commandment of Jesus thus becomes a descriptive rather than an ethical mandate. Jesus, the incarnate God, touches children, women, Samaritans, prisoners, lepers, Pharisees, Roman centurions, fishermen, Jews and Gentiles. Jesus embodies the Divine through love. 1 Corinthians 12 and 13 reinforces our interconnection and the primacy of grace and love for one another that are borne from the Divine.

Proposed Ethical Response

An ethical response that strives to focus on the touch of God through inter-human relationships will no doubt begin to tear down the social constructs of difference that separate humans from one another and from God. How might the mission team turn their transformational experiences in Africa into faithful Christian ethical responses? First, the team could choose to maintain monthly e-mail exchanges with their African friends and continue to nurture a mutual relationship by carefully listening to how they could engage in a mutual exchange of tangible resources with their African mission partners. For example, they might make it possible for their African friends to travel to the U.S. to share their faith and lead in worship. This would offer opportunities for faith conversations with the entire Houston congregation such as they had in Africa that were so transformational.

Second, the pastor, Linda, could offer a series of sermons and/or Bible studies around the new question she had added to the mission team's daily devotional time in Africa ("How is God calling the Christian church to bear witness in the globalized disparity of wealth and poverty?"). She could begin to lead the Houston congregation to reflect critically on how their faith intersects with the pressures they experience of racism, domestic violence,

9. Rivera, *Touch of Transcendence*, 123.

food insecurity, sexual orientation bias, workplace wage theft and other inequities. Linda could build on this collective theological conversation to help the church re-envision how it engages with *all* recipients of their charitable mission work. She could guide congregants towards a mutual relationship with the persons they serve by helping them listen to and see others as people with problem solving skills, personal stories and faith experiences to share.

William Kincaid

Entering the Case at the Intersection of Minister and Experience

At the heart of ministerial and theological reflection is a deep, dynamic commitment to be present in and to an experience in ministry and to remain open to the larger questions of faith and ministry. Doing so involves sustained engagement and hopeful interplay between courage and vulnerability. To illustrate this, let me begin by noting both Pastor Linda's question and Corey's first response.

Consider Pastor Linda's question: "How is God calling the Christian church to bear witness in the globalized disparity of wealth and poverty?" If this is a genuine inquiry—that is, if Pastor Linda's needs have not unduly influenced her motivation for asking the question—it demonstrates remarkable nerve. Do any of us dare to ponder in any serious way what God requires of us? Voicing such a question involves intense vulnerability. After all, genuine questions often lead to inconvenient and even costly answers along the journey of faith. I see signs of Pastor Linda demonstrating courage and vulnerability not only through her participation in these mission trips and the pre-education she has offered for them, but also by being told that these experiences have caused her to explore new theological understanding for the sake of her continued pastoral leadership. Pastor Linda is not asking the group to do anything that she is not also doing herself.

I see similar dynamics at play with Corey, who "ventured a response." To venture a response signals an indefinite path, an uncertain outcome and the kind of groping that characterizes a good deal of discernment and discipleship. I venture, as Corey did, from the standpoint of vulnerability, recognizing that I may make incorrect assumptions, work from an incomplete pictures, and offer proposals that will need continued refinement and experimentation. And yet, as I see in Corey's willingness to enter into the conversation, to venture is to embody courage. It is to utter possibilities and invoke worlds that may seem fanciful and preposterous to many, including those who will seek to silence his speech because they will rightly hear his utterances as unsettling and threatening.

Making Meaning at the Intersection of Gospel and Context

Mission trips typically provide encounters between people from radically different contexts. They usually expose faith commitments and other values that have remained implicit to that point. Such is the case when the upper middle class Americans from a suburban Houston church make their annual visit to a Kenyan village where global economic policies have exacerbated pressing local challenges to a nearly unbearable point.

Recent critiques of mission trips in general have raised awareness of how missioners frequently privilege certain assumptions, social locations and faith perspectives. This case presents several opportunities to ask questions both of the Christian story and the context (or contexts in this as in most cases), and to bring them into conversation with each other.[10] I do so with the hope that ministerial reflection not only benefits the minister's understanding and practice, but also helps those in the minister's care develop a Christian interpretation of the world and their place in it.

For example, Pastor Linda's question—"How is God calling the Christian church to bear witness in the globalized disparity of wealth and poverty?"—holds the gospel and the context before the group and essentially asks, 'What do these two things, gospel and context, have to do with each other?' 'How do they inform, challenge and interpret each other?' The dialogue in the latter half of the case represents the kind of grappling that a minister (or any other person of faith) craves. Everyone jumped into the conversation, each one weighting gospel and context a little differently.

Regarding an understanding of context, I find Pastor Linda's view that past participants "lacked any political or economic analysis" as fairly surprising. It sounds like an exaggeration born of frustration, perhaps even some projection of the pastor's own prior lack of understanding onto the group members. Many upper-middle class whites in the United States are at least somewhat familiar with the basics of global economics, if for no

---

10. For a superb example of this interplay between gospel and context, see Walter Brueggemann's reflections on faith and anxiety in ancient Egypt and the United States in Brueggmann, *Journey*, 1–36.

other reason than to retain their place on the economic ladder. This might describe Jim, who interrupted Sheila with the animated announcement that politics, religion and money don't mix. There is no surer way to maintain the status quo than to keep such things compartmentalized, to keep gospel and context as far from each other as the east is from the west or, as in this case, as far as the "technological, therapeutic, consumer militarism that socializes all Americans"[11] is from Kenya's landscapes with its stunning wildlife and heartbreaking poverty.

Regarding the gospel, part of the work of ministerial reflection is to clarify the theological assumptions and sources at play, both during the pastor's reflection on her own experience and for the community of which she is a part. So, for instance, I wonder what claims Corey is making when he references what seems like an easy default: the story of the cleansing of the temple found in Matthew 21 and John 2. While an important story that exposes the perversion of worship through economic transaction, words of the prophets put a sharper point on the issue. Consider the word of judgment in Micah 3:9 against those "who abhor justice and pervert all equity." Amos 4:1 warns that those who oppress the poor and crush the needy will surely meet with their own destruction eventually. These examples critique the context of globalized economics with a faith story passionate about justice.

Sheila's use of a plural possessive pronoun raises an interesting angle. She says that she does not feel guilty for "our blessings," which calls for some probing into exactly who is included in "our." It seems clear that she sees her own affluence as a sign of God's providence or favor. The "our" could refer as well to the team members present on the mission trip or to the relative wealth known by many in the United States. Sheila is making a statement about the nature of God, but also about the context in which she lives. It appears she may be allowing the comfort of her context to take the upper hand in interpreting the gospel rather than asking the gospel to critique her social location.

Toward A Faithful Response: Putting Resources and Strategies Together

Most pastors and congregations analyze and diagnose situations but stop short of the treacherous ground where specific steps are named and

---

11. Brueggemann, *Mandate*, 63.

concrete priorities are adopted. In this case, Pastor Linda is guiding a provocative conversation in which the mission team members are beginning to ask the same question the crowds asked of John the Baptist, "What then shall we do?" (Luke 3:10). Killen and de Beer describe this aspect of reflection as "searching for a way to be faithful."[12]

This part of the process of reflection revolves around resources and strategies and I see signs of engagement with those two things immediately. Pastor Linda has drawn on the resources of her own experiences and reflections in Kenya, as well as engaging the perspectives of liberation and postcolonial theologians. From that deeper understanding she developed a strategy to provide information prior to the trip about the effects of the globalized economic and political institutions in Kenya. In addition to the educational materials, she also added a bold question for the group's devotion time: "How is God calling the Christian church to bear witness in the globalized disparity of wealth and poverty?" We should not discount the resources of prayer and shared wisdom in such a scenario, but this very question calls for action.

Grace and Mark also quickly turn to resources and strategies, raising opportunities like buying Fair Trade tea, building relationships at a homeless shelter, and making globalization work for the whole world and not just a privileged few. The economic status of the team members, on the one hand, should position them to use their various resources and connections to influence decisions that would positively impact Kenyans and others, but often those same resources entrap people at a certain level of lifestyle and prevent them from advocating for a broader distribution of resources to those who would most benefit.

A common pitfall, especially when the differential of material resources is great, is to assume that those with less have nothing to offer. I see signs of the prosperous and healthy benefitting the impoverished and ill through building a new dormitory. What a gift! In this case, however, the Kenyans may have given the most precious resource of all—hospitality. Through their genuine and deeply felt hospitality, the Kenyans happened to give the gift that the Americans most needed, which is the space and stillness in which to observe, listen and learn from others. In the mutuality of those burgeoning relationships, the church members entered into moments of vulnerability and discovery that they might otherwise guard

12. For a helpful discussion on entering and re-entering our experience, see Killen and de Beer, *The Art of Theological Reflection*, 22–27.

against when they are at home in the suburbs of the United States. In the safety of that mutuality members of the mission team can begin thinking concretely about strategies.

Pastor Linda closes the reflection with the somewhat awkward announcement that Corey is right, a strategy that can undermine a group process and shut down continued exploration and discernment. As with any reflective process, I am privy to a particular frame of this event, but not all of it. Perhaps this is the point at which the conversation for this mission team and the congregation picks up next time.

QUESTIONS FOR DISCUSSION

1. Is your own approach to theological reflection grounded in any particular theology, as Docampo's is grounded in postcolonial theology?

2. (How) does theological reflection help you "develop a Christian interpretation of the world and [your] place in it"?

BIBLIOGRAPHY

Browning, Don S. *A Fundamental Practical Theology: Descriptive and Strategic Proposals.* Minneapolis: Fortress, 1996.

Brueggemann, Walter. *Journey to the Common Good.* Louisville: Westminster John Knox, 2010.

———. *Mandate to Difference: An Invitation to the Contemporary Church.* Louisville: Westminster John Knox, 2007.

Keller, Catherine, Michael Nausner, and Mayra Rivera, eds. *Postcolonial Theologies: Divinity and Empire.* St. Louis: Chalice, 2004.

Killen, Patricia O'Connell, and John de Beer. *The Art of Theological Reflection.* New York: Crossroad, 1994.

Pui-lan, Kwok. *Postcolonial Feminist Theology and Imagination.* Louisville: Westminster John Knox, 2005.

Raheb, Mitri. *Faith in the Face of Empire: The Bible through Palestinian Eyes.* Maryknoll, NY: Orbis, 2014.

Rivera, Mayra. *The Touch of Transcendence: A Postcolonial Theology of God.* Louisville: Westminster John Knox, 2007.

Said, Edward. *Orientalism.* New York: Random House, 1978.

Spivak, Gayatri Chakravorty. *Death of a Discipline.* New York: Columbia University Press, 2003.

10

So This Is Ministry?

Richard Cunningham and George Hillman

INTRODUCTION

Cunningham:

BOTH THE CHARACTER IN this case and the reader of it will discover that it is a good thing to be perplexed, because perplexity raises curiosity. Without curiosity, there would be no inquiry, no further exploration. Reflecting on a case is an opportunity to clarify meanings, uncover values, and give nuance to the responses, actions, theories, theologies, and roles of the pastoral person.

At the same time, sometimes reflection processes can appear excessively multifaceted and cumbersome. In an effort to cut to the heart of the matter, I employ a threefold method of provocative questions. Simply stated the model is:

- *What?*
- *So What?*
- *Now What?*

These words are easy to recall, but as is, the model is anemic, and we want to develop the muscle of curiosity, the heart of engagement, and the ear of listening. So let us expand it.

What? means: What would people in the case become aware of, if they were more self-aware? Here we focus on dominant thoughts, feelings, and impressions in the case, its sensate elements (touch, smell, sound, taste), and its ambiguities and tensions. What would people in the case become aware of if they were more aware of their relationship to others? We look for what triangles or patterns are present, what the social and cultural location of the case suggests about relationship, and what power dynamics are operating.

So What? invites reflectors to ask: What is holy or sacred in the case? How does the incident correlate or intersect with the sacred? How is the deity present? What symbols, images, and metaphors stand out? What sacred writings or traditions come to mind? What is the sacred theme? What is the heart of the matter?

When we ask *Now What?* we are asking after what new thing might emerge from the case. What needs to be reframed?

Hillman:

The theological reflection model I will be using works through four resources available to a Christian: Christian Scripture, Christian Heritage, Cultural Experience, and Personal Experience. From these four resources, I make the final step of application.[1]

3. *Christian Scripture.* The revelatory starting point of the Bible is a foundation of the reflection.[2] Questions to ask here include whether there are specific biblical passages, persons, or themes that addresses the experience in the case.

4. *Christian Heritage.* Christian tradition is rich with insights from brothers and sisters in the faith who have gone before us.[3] Some questions to consider are these: How have other Christians in history dealt with the same issue? What insights or solutions can be found in church history that address the situation of the case?

---

1. This model is explained more fully in Hillman, *Ministry Greenhouse.*
2. Grenz and Olson, *Who Needs Theology?*, 95.
3. Ibid., 96.

5. *Cultural Experience.* Culture helps explain how a particular heritage and setting (religious, ethnic, political, economic, media environment, and traditions) develop a person's convictions, values, beliefs, biases, understanding of reality, and expectations of appropriate behavior.[4]

6. *Personal Experience.* Just as no one ministers in a cultural vacuum, no one ministers in a personal vacuum either. Personal experiences make all of us who we are today. Questions to address here include how a person has responded to similar situations in the past and how they were taught growing up, especially regarding issues of conflict, leadership, and communication.

7. *Application.* Theological reflection is ultimately a call to application in life. Relevant questions in the final steps may consist of any of the following:

   a. What are the questions that still linger for the reflector? What feelings remain raw, unprocessed, or unsettled for the reflector?

   b. What present beliefs or actions need to change? What should we do differently in the future?

   c. What has been learned about the self, others, and, above all, God?

   d. How will God work in this situation or in future situations?

On a personal note, let me say that I was immediately drawn to this case for two reasons. First, I have seen plenty of Michaels at my seminary. As our student population continues to shift to more non-traditional demographics, more "second career" students are leaving successful careers to enter the uncharted waters of vocational ministry. It is actually quite exciting to see Michaels entering the field.

But I was also drawn to this case because I too am a doer who struggles at times with slowing down for the ministry of presence. There are many times when I find myself driving the ministry (wanting results) rather than slowing down and just being with my people. In today's culture of accomplishment where success is measured by what is achieved, this is a risk most of us face at one time or another. And when a person is leaving years in the corporate world behind to enter vocational ministry, that shift can be especially jarring.

4. Lynne DeLay and Maxine Dalton, "Coaching," in Ting and Scisco, eds., *The CCL Handbook*, 125.

THE CASE

Context

As a computer programmer working for a major Silicon Valley firm Michael had risen to the top of his profession but was very unhappy. He was a no-nonsense, get it done now, kind of guy. He had always wanted to be a pastor, so at age 42 he entered a seminary in his city. The master's degree program required a yearlong internship which was intended to challenge his comfort zone—meaning a different social, cultural, economic and ecclesial environment. Michael chose to work in a local church whose mission was to work with people who lived in the immediate neighborhood.

The Event

Michael was eager to talk with his internship supervisor, the Rev. Marion Monroe. Michael dominated the conversation in Pastor Monroe's unpretentious office on the second floor. He said, "Thursday began when you showed me the setup for the bazaar. You will recall that we chatted with some of the women who had come in to set up and decorate, and you introduced me to a few of them."

Pastor Monroe listened carefully, nodding with understanding and encouraging Michael to continue to express his observations and concerns. Michael continued, "As we headed for the office to work on planning a program together, I recall saying that it was time to end our playing and get to work, and you responded that what we had been doing was our work—it was ministry. I'm not quite sure how it was ministry; you keep talking about a 'ministry of presence,' but I'm never sure when my presence is a ministry and when it is just presence."

Michael was conflicted; he wanted results now and had little patience for small talk, and some of these people who lived in the neighborhood dressed poorly, smelled bad, and didn't seem to track a simple conversation. Michael thought there needed to be a systematic program to follow rather than this ministry of presence.

Michael left the church that afternoon perplexed about what Pastor Monroe said about a "ministry of presence." He was left wondering what that meant. Is that what Jesus did? How do you know if you're successful? Shouldn't I be leading a Bible study or something more spiritual?

REFLECTION

George Hillman

Christian Scripture

In hearing Michael's struggle, I am immediately drawn to the story of Mary and Martha in Luke 10:38–42, where Martha is distracted, anxious, and troubled with "all her preparations" [NASB] while Mary chooses the one necessary thing, the "good part." Michael is a Martha, a person of action wishing to do great things for the Lord (which is a noble thing). But the better thing is to stop and listen to what Jesus is saying in the midst of all of the busyness. The internship supervisor Rev. Monroe is trying to encourage Michael to enter a Mary mode of slowing down and just being present. You can almost imagine Martha saying the very words spoken by Michael in this case: "Let's "end our playing and get to work." Michael needs to be reminded that our busyness does not make us holy.

Besides slowing down to practice a ministry of presence, I also hear echoes of calls for compassion in this case. It is implied Michael is likely serving in a poorer neighborhood (at least poorer than what Michael is used to). Michael (as all believers in Jesus) is called to compassionate love of others. As the Lord is compassionate and gracious, so those who minster are to be the same (Mic 6:8). God cares for widows and orphans and by implication all who are neglected by society (Deut 10:18; 24:17). God clearly gives justice to the needy and requires that of His servants (Exod 23:6–11; Lev 19:10; Pss 70:4; 86:1; Prov 14:31). Michael needs to be reminded it is for these very people (the ones who dress poorly, are smelly, and are simple thinkers) that he has been called to minister in the name of Jesus.

Christian Heritage

A saint of old who speaks of the ministry of presence is St. Gregory the Great (540- 604 AD) in his foundational work, *The Book of Pastoral Rule.*[5] In training up new pastors who were not unlike Michael, Gregory encouraged them to love others, for the pastor's voice "more easily penetrates his listeners' hearts when his way of life commends what he says."[6] Michael needs to be reminded that he must know his sheep before he can speak into

5. Gregory the Great, *Pastoral Rule.*

6. Ibid., 51.

the lives of his sheep. This goes for both the volunteers Michael is working with and the people in the neighborhood. Gregory also encouraged new pastors to find a balance between compassion for the neighbor and time away for contemplation, "Otherwise, in pursuing high things he will despise the infirmities of his neighbor, or by adapting himself to the infirmities of his neighbors he will abandon the pursuit of high things."[7] Gregory would also tell new pastors like Michael, "Doctrine does not penetrate the mind of the needy if the hand of compassion does not commend it to the soul. But the seed of the Word does grow well, when the kindness of the preacher waters it in the heart of his audience."[8] Michael needs to be reminded that he is there to build people (both the volunteers and the neighborhood) and not just to accomplish tasks, because the people *are* the ministry.

Cultural Experience

As we shift to cultural experience, the first words that jump off of the page are that Michael worked for a "major Silicon Valley firm." Michael has most likely been living for several years in a very affluent, fast paced and success-driven part of the country where entrepreneurs and techies are elevated for what they accomplish. This Silicon Valley culture must have influenced Michael in at least two ways. First, Michael had probably succeeded in a very fast paced tech economy by his hard work and hustle. He was probably rewarded for getting things done. Now he has shifted into vocational ministry, where tangible markers of success are subtler. How does a minister *quantify* a changed life? Where are the numbers that measure whether a minister is being successful in a church? Is it even about numbers and task accomplishment at all? Or does Michael need to realize that there is a mystery at work in ministry? Michael wants to "end our playing and get to work." Michael wants a "systematic program" because (most likely) that type of program is what brought him success and significance in his previous career. Michael needs to be reminded that what worked in Silicon Valley does not work in his new context—and may not even be biblical.

As a byproduct of having risen to the top at a Silicon Valley firm, Michael probably enjoyed the material blessings that come from a successful career in the tech industry. Though the case does not confirm this, one has to wonder whether Michael hasn't been well off financially before coming

7. Ibid., 58.
8. Ibid., 72.

to seminary. Now he is ministering to a population that may be outside his comfort zone—people in the neighborhood that "dressed poorly, smelled bad, and didn't seem to track a simple conversation." Could this even be Michael's first real interaction with poverty? Michael needs to be reminded that there is great opportunity for personal growth in compassionate love in his own life as he allows God to use him in the lives of others.

Personal Experience

In the case, Michael is described as a "no-nonsense, get it done now, kind of guy." Again, Michael wants to "end our playing and get to work." Michael **"wanted results now and had little patience for small talk."** How much of this comes from traits he cultivated in order to be successful while employed in Silicon Valley and how much of this is a description of his personality? Someone needs to have a conversation with Michael about what drives him to get things done and to get results. Is this a healthy "can do" attitude that just needs to be tempered or is there more to be revealed in his life story explaining why he is so driven (such as trying to please parents growing up, or achievement drivers in school). Whatever the conversation suggests, Michael needs to be reminded that his identity is not wrapped up in what he accomplishes.

We also read that Michael "dominated the conversation" with Rev. Monroe. This cannot be overlooked. Is this another part of his personality that just needs tempering, the corporate culture speaking through him so that he needs to unlearn old ways, or is there an issue with gender bias here? Michael is working with a woman supervisor and with women volunteers. Has he had positive previous experiences with a woman supervisor before or with working with women in his office? In addition to the conversation about being driven, Michael might benefit from a conversation about his view of women in the workplace and in ministry. Michael may need to be reminded of the value of women.

Application

QUESTIONS THAT LINGER

I have asked many questions throughout my reflection. Ideally, I would want them answered before offering concrete suggestions as to what Michael might do in the future. In particular, as a "doer" myself who is sympathetic to the challenges of slowing down, I would want to know more about how success was defined for him growing up and in his previous employment. One feeling that remains raw for me as a reflector is how past definitions of success so greatly affect future ministry.

BELIEFS AND ACTIONS NEEDING CHANGE

Michael needs to be willing to enter into the ministry of presence that is being encouraged by Rev. Monroe. I am sure Michael is a capable manager and Bible teacher, but the task at hand is calling for a new skill, that of being present with both volunteers and the people in the neighborhood. Michael needs to learn this soft skill of pastoral care, a skill that cannot be learned from a book or lecture. My hope is that by placing himself in situations where *only* a ministry of presence is required, he will allow the Holy Spirit to soften his heart toward people.

NEW LEARNING ABOUT SELF, OTHERS, AND GOD

I would hope the disequilibrium Michael is feeling would make him willing to take a look at his own life and its driven quality. How much of his desire to get tasks done is healthy? How much of his drive is based on his desire for significance or acceptance? I would hope Michael would begin to see life through a lens of grace (toward himself and others) rather than a lens of a project list. Most important, I would hope Michael would learn about the compassionate love of God as the Holy Spirit uses him to be an instrument of grace in the lives of others.

HOW GOD WILL WORK: ISSUES OF TRUST

Finally, this case is ultimately an issue of trust. Is Michael going to trust in his own efforts at the church, or is he willing to trust Rev. Monroe this time? In this case, Michael is not the one in charge. Michael needs to learn to become a follower before he can become a leader of God's people. More important, is Michael going to trust in his own efforts at the church or is Michael willing to trust God for the results? God is at work in the lives of the volunteers and in the lives of the people they are ministering to in the neighborhood. Is Michael going to miss seeing God at work by being so busy trying to accomplish things for God?

Richard Cunningham

What? (Self-Awareness)

Michael is ready to go! He is a high achiever. Give him a task, rules and the right language, and he will finish the task and do it right. The church bazaar and Michael's image of ministry are in tension. He experiences a disconnect from his spirituality, his role as a pastoral leader, and his image of God. The disconnect becomes the key to opening the door to exploration and learning.

Michael clearly does not comprehend either internally or externally the meaning of a *ministry of presence*. For him, just meeting other people is insufficient without something concrete like a Bible study or a spiritual discussion. He has the image of success he had as a computer programmer.

There is a cultural divide between Michael and the persons in the church's neighborhood. He is not aware of his own cultural distance, position of privilege, and discomfort with those who live on the margins.

At an interior level Michael's feels mystified and conflicted. He is no longer at the center of the relationship, the one in charge, or the leader.

What? (Awareness of Self in Relationship to/with Others)

Pastor Monroe presents herself as accessible to Michael and willing to listen to his concerns. She views ministry differently than Michael. She values "being with the other" rather than "doing something *to* the other." Her desire is to be a pastor, one who stands with those on the outside. She thereby offers a different view of justice, as well.

Michael, on the other hand, is looking for a systematic way to present his religious understanding to the people of the church. As in his prior work environment, doing something concrete and getting results is a highly prized value.

We can interpret Michael's relationship to others through the lens of several possible triangles among *Perpetrator*, *Victim*, and *Rescuer* in this case. One triangle might be this:

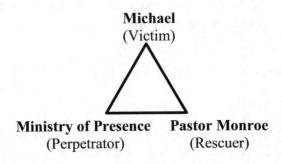

Michael
(Victim)

Ministry of Presence
(Perpetrator)

Pastor Monroe
(Rescuer)

If Michael views himself as *Victim,* that means he thinks of himself as someone not up to the task. He stands alone. He does not understand his purpose or function in this new environment. He is very uncomfortable. He feels threatened by being a "minister of presence" (the *Perpetrator*) something he knows nothing about. He wants for Pastor Monroe to *rescue* him.

Another triangle might be:

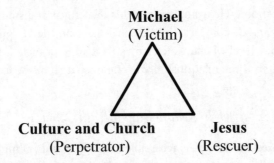

Michael
(Victim)

Culture and Church
(Perpetrator)

Jesus
(Rescuer)

In this rendering of the relationships, the church is alien to Michael because it's located in a different culture; neither the church nor the culture is one he knows. He desperately wants to be *rescued* by Jesus.

And still another triangle might be:

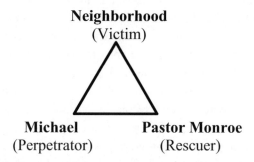

Neighborhood
(Victim)

Michael   **Pastor Monroe**
(Perpetrator)   (Rescuer)

Michael views the neighborhood as depressed. It looks, smells, tastes, and feels different than where he lives. He places himself above the people in the neighborhood, where he believes there is no hope. From his position of privilege, he has the answers—if they would only go to school, work harder, pick up the trash. Because Pastor Monroe has been at the church for a while, she will tell him what to do.

So What? (Theological Framework)

The context of Michael's internship becomes a crucible for him as he finds himself having to explore and clarify his theological assumptions, prejudices and opinions. He is working out of a framework that Patricia O'Connell Killen and John de Beer identify as "the standpoint of certitude." They write, "From this standpoint we see the unfamiliar only in terms of what we already believe. From certitude we can tolerate only that which fits our predetermined categories."[9] Michael may not even be aware of those categories; however, he has held them for a very long time.

As he ponders his new role as a minister meeting people who are setting up and decorating for a church bazaar, his concept of ministry dissolves. He believes he is supposed to do something "spiritual," something godly. This approach cuts into his self-understanding and personal discomfort meeting others and sharing personal stories.

Michael has most likely learned a "religious code language," which is extremely useful with those who know the language. It works within families, work environments, and other socio-cultural settings where people know one another. Code language is deemed valuable in discussion groups,

9. Killen and de Beer, *The Art of Theological Reflection*, 4.

worship, sermons and scripture study. On the one hand, it creates inclusivity. However, it can be off-putting to those who do not know the code.

Michael views himself as a spiritual leader and is certain that God is with him. As such, he believes he is the one who holds essential information and truths that others must hear. Although he does not want to admit it, he believes 'the other' does not have God. Michael is responsible for taking God to them. What would it be like for Michael to explore the idea that the poor and smelly people could reveal God to *him*?

Rev. Monroe presents a different pastoral model for Michael to consider—a ministry of presence which means simply being with the other and not *doing* something to them. A ministry of presence suggests that God is accessible, available to all. God, if God is love, is revealed in the person who comes to the bazaar as well as to Michael.

God is discovered and disclosed in the mystery of the interaction. Theologian Martin Buber articulates this in the expression "I-Thou."[10] He defines an "I–it" relationship as one that objectifies the other. In this case, the "it" are "poorly dressed, smell bad, and don't seem to track a simple conversation." The "I-Thou" relationship occurs where the other is not separated by discrete boundaries. One is invited to sit at the bazaar table and find nourishment in conversation and the breaking of bread.

The parables of Jesus model a ministry of presence. The parables do not yield black and white images; rather, they disclose possibilities by inviting the curious to explore the unexpected and ponder the mystery—yeast in flour, seed in soil, light in darkness. We are left with curiosity and wonder at the bazaar table. What does it mean to break open the bread of hospitality and the cup of new life with those in the neighborhood?

Now What? (Praxis)

What emerges that might shape Michael, his future, and his pastoral practice? What is generated that will inform, direct, and lead him into the future?[11] Michael would benefit from clarifying his pastoral stance,

---

10. Buber, *I and Thou.*

11. Joe Holland and Peter Henriot S.J., identify this moment as the final point on the "pastoral circle" and call it "pastoral planning." Pastoral planning involves asking: "In light of experiences analyzed and reflected upon, what response is called for by individuals and by communities?" In Holland and Henriot, *Social Analysis,* 9.

reframing his image of self, reimaging his image of God, and exploring the biblical notion of a faith that does justice.

Michael's struggle is to discover his identity as a pastor in a new context. It is the struggle of many pastors, chaplains, and church leaders, lay or ordained. The turning point in this case happens when Michael sits down with Pastor Monroe to discuss the concept of 'ministry of presence.' In that moment, he is challenged to re-think and re-image his conceptual frameworks.

Truly understanding what it means to offer a ministry of presence begins when one appreciates it as an art form developed over time with a great deal of practice and reflection. It is not a step-by-step process with scriptures to quote, words to say, or methods to use. Becoming an empathetic pastoral presence is not something that one memorizes or puts on like a new dress or suit. It is not a particular set of skills one 'gets right' as in a medical model of listening and diagnosing. Nevertheless, there are some images and concepts that are helpful to remember as one is learning what it means to become a pastoral presence.

We can imagine Pastor Monroe counseling Michael in several ways. 'Wait with someone when there is no more waiting within you.' 'Discover that it is not about you.' 'Recognize the God within the other rather than thinking you are bringing God to the other.' 'Engage the theology of the other rather than presenting yours or correcting theirs.' 'Place your emotions or feelings in a safe container while giving the other time to speak theirs without judgment.' 'Know the difference between sympathy and empathy.' 'Be willing to sit with the other in the not-knowing when you don't know what to say.' 'Uncover your hearing so that listening is more important than talking.' 'Find that rescuing is less important than understanding the other's truth.' 'Determine that the invitation to pray is an opportunity to invite the other to pray with you.' 'Encourage the other to ponder the Jesus question 'Where is your treasure?.'' 'Remember that active listening takes time and that the discovery or recovery of the other's story is essential.'

QUESTION FOR DISCUSSION

1. Have you ever found theological reflection "cumbersome," as Cunningham suggests it can sometimes become? How have you simplified it?

BIBLIOGRAPHY

Buber, Martin. *I and Thou*. Translated by Ronald Gregor Smith. New York: Scribner, 2000.

Gregory the Great. *The Book of Pastoral Rule*. Translated by George Demacopoulos. Crestwood, NY: St. Vladimir's Seminary, 2007.

Grenz, Stanley, and Roger Olson. *Who Needs Theology? An Invitation to the Study of God*. Downers Grove, IL: InterVarsity, 1996.

Hillman, George. *Ministry Greenhouse: Cultivating Environments for Practical Learning*. Herndon, VA: Alban Institute, 2008.

Holland, Joe, and Peter Henriot, SJ. *Social Analysis: Linking Faith and Justice*. Rev. and enl. ed. Maryknoll, NY: Orbis, 1983.

Killen, Patricia O'Connell, and John de Beer. *The Art of Theological Reflection*. New York: Crossroad, 1994.

Ting, Sharon, and Peter Scisco, eds. *The CCL Handbook of Coaching: A Guide for the Leader Coach*. San Francisco: Jossey-Bass, 2006.

11

Which Religion Is Better?

Joseph E. Bush and Sue Withers

INTRODUCTION

Bush:

FOR MY REFLECTION, I utilize my own "practical hermeneutics grid" for facilitating cross-cultural communication.[1] The grid is designed to help us to attend to multiple interpretations that might be possible when hearing confusing or puzzling statements from speakers in pastoral situations, or even when confronting 'hot button' phrases in theological discussions. The method is neither meant to establish the right meaning of a phrase in an absolute sense nor even the intended meaning of the speaker with any certainty. It is meant to help us in pastoral encounters to access multiple meanings in a phrase and then choose a generous interpretation and response toward the speaker.

---

1. I had originally developed the grid working with chaplains and CPE supervisors in a hospital system in Minnesota who were dealing with cultural and theological diversity, and I subsequently refined it further with the Australian New Zealand Association of Theological Field Educators. I am indebted to Fr. John Chalmers for helping me refine the method. For more information, see Bush, "What Island Are You From?" The practical hermeneutics grid is also explained further in my forthcoming book, *Practical Theology in Church and Society*.

The method begins by identifying the phrase in question and brain-storming possible meanings that might be intended by the speaker, as well as different meanings the phrase might already hold for the listener. Meanings already held can sometimes interfere with our ability to discern the speaker's intent; alternatively, they can provide points of possible contact in communication between us. The method asks us next to notice the possible similarities and differences between us when we compare our respective sets of possible meanings. It then has us brainstorm possible responses open to us and, finally, to choose from among them that which seems most 'generous' toward the other. The method also asks us to notice contextual factors shaping the situation and framing the possible interpretations and responses.

In my reflection I refer to myself in the first person because I was the author of and preacher in the case.

Withers:

I employ a transcendental method of John Paver.[2] He developed it as an adaptation of previous models: "The source of the transcendental model is in the work of [Stephen B.] Bevans and theologians Bernard Lonergan and Sallie McFague but has been further developed by myself . . . I have developed and refined this model because of the way other models neglect inner experience and spirituality. The transcendental model attends to spirituality without neglecting critical analysis, social justice, and the need for change."[3] Paver contrasts the transcendental model of theological reflection with two other familiar ones: *the ministry model* of the Whiteheads, and *the praxis model* of Joe Holland and Peter Henriot. The former, he says, privileges reflection that leads to action within a certain ministerial context, and the latter emphasizes liberation from oppression. The transcendental model prioritizes the reflector's inner experience. Paver quotes Bevans: "Rather, the starting point is transcendental, concerned with one's own religious experience and one's own experience of oneself."[4]

The method moves through four stages that I follow in my reflection, though I reverse the second and third.[5]

2. Paver, *Theological Reflection*.

3. Ibid., 65–66.

4. Bevans, *Contextual Theology*, as quoted in Paver, *Theological Reflection*, 67.

5. Paver, *Theological Reflection*, 78: Fig. 2.5.

1. *Beginning with the authentic self*

   The self is always determined by cultural heritage, history, family, religious experience, etc.

2. *Working through self-deception*

   The reflector has to acknowledge self-deception, which is claiming either too much or too little for oneself.[6]

3. *Conversation partners*

   All ministries and lives have themes that become partners in the conversation that is theological reflection. Conversation partners can also include unexpected additional 'selves.'[7]

4. *New horizons and new action*

   Having been open to God's revelation within human experience, the reflector seeks renewed commitment to God and people.

My use of Paver's transcendental method places me imaginatively within the case itself, conversing with the congregant.

Bush and Withers, writing together about their collaboration:

We were each pleasantly struck with a sense that our methods and our reflections seemed to complement each other. Both of our methods are honoring the realities of distanciation in hermeneutics, which can be especially noticeable in the differences between speaker and listener in cross-cultural encounter. Sue's use of John Paver's transcendental method focuses more on her own internal process as the listener. Joe's method attempts to name some of the assumptions that might be filtering his hearing, and then to move to speculate broadly about the various possibilities that might be intended by the speaker. Combined, our contributions illustrate something of the pastoral challenge to develop self-awareness in order to focus attention authentically on others. Ironically such self-awareness is necessary for being able to hear others with deeper respect and appreciation. It's possible to miss this balance in either direction—either by becoming self-absorbed or by blithely interacting without either self-awareness or sensitivity. We find in each other's reflections here a modeling of the attempt to find this

---

6. Paver says that in theological reflection, the temptation is to lay claim to too many strengths as a person and a pastor. Paver, *Theological Reflection*, 69.

7. Ibid., 72–73.

proper balance. We use different means in this endeavor—Sue giving more time to self-reflection in order to engage respectfully, Joe giving more time to the attempt to hear the other in order to posture himself authentically in relation with him. In retrospect, it is interesting to us that both of us focused more on personal and interpersonal dimensions of this case than on explicit theological language. Each in our own way, we are attending to the challenge of hearing and responding within the broader context of cross-cultural relationships.

THE CASE

Context

The immediate context of this case is a field trip in which I took my students from the Pacific Theological College in Fiji to some rural villages on a neighboring island in Fiji. The students were Pacific Islanders from Samoa, Tonga, Vanuatu, and Solomon Islands as well as Fiji. I am of European decent.

The wider context is that of Fiji, a nation almost evenly divided between two distinct demographic groups. Half the population is Indigenous Melanesians who are overwhelmingly Christian and predominantly Methodist. The other half of the population are East Indians—an enduring legacy of the indentured labor system during British colonialism—who are primarily Hindu and Muslim. At the time of the field trip, the nation was engaged in drafting a Constitution and was embroiled in debate about its religious identity. Many indigenous Melanesians wanted the Constitution to declare Fiji to be a Christian nation even while protecting religious liberty. Many East Indians were very worried about the implications of such Christian nationalism.

The Event

According to custom, the highest ranking in status delivers the message when invited for the first time to a village. That's why I was the preacher that day. It happened to also be "Prophet Muhammad's Birthday" on the Fijian calendar which celebrated Christian, Hindu and Muslim holidays as well as both British and Fijian national ones. Fijians like holidays. Even though there were no Muslims present within this village, I thought this was still a good occasion for making some theological connections between Muslims and Christians, two communities that had been experiencing tension within the nation.

I preached on Mark 9:40 ("Whoever is not against us is for us") and on the blessing of Ishmael in Genesis 17:20 and 21:17–18. From memory, I mentioned some of the statements about Jesus that are made in the Qur'an— those proclaiming Jesus' virgin birth and ascension, and declaring that he is the messiah, word of God and having a spirit from God.[8] I acknowledged the differences between the two religions, especially pertaining to the Trinity, but I emphasized their similarity as Abrahamic religions that believed in one God and confessed a similar heritage. I thought I preached pretty well. Afterward, a congregant asked me sincerely, "So which is better?" "Better?" I inquired for elaboration. "Yes," he clarified, "which religion is better?" My initial impression was that he was ready to consider converting to Islam. However, as a visitor I knew I could not trust first impressions. I knew one has to question one's own inferences.

REFLECTION

Joseph E. Bush

Practical Hermeneutics Grid For Facilitating Cross-Cultural Communication

Phrase in Question	
Possible meanings **the speaker** might bring	Possible meanings I, **the listener**, might bring (both intellectually and viscerally)
Possible **similarities** between us	Possible **differences** between us
My possible **responses** to this phrase	Which of my possible responses would be **most generous** to the speaker
Contextual/cultural factors shaping the meanings in the encounter	

The puzzling phrase in question for me in this case is the question posed by the congregant following the sermon: "Which religion is better?"

8. See Qur'an 2:87; 3:45–47; 3:49; 3:55; 4:158; 4:171.

Contextual/cultural factors

Let us start at the bottom of the grid and address the contextual and cultural factors in this case first, since they are important to understanding
the case. First, the temporal situation in which event of this case takes
place is a pastoral encounter. This is one of those short encounters following worship. On top of that, I am a guest preacher in this congregation, with
little chance for subsequent follow-up with my speaker. I inhabit other roles
besides preacher: I am a guest in this village and I am a teacher accompanying students from other island nations.

Second, several cross-cultural factors frame this encounter. Fiji is
marked by racial, cultural and religious diversity. In this case, the speaker
and the listener (me) are both residents of Fiji, but the speaker is an indigenous resident of this rural village and I am an immigrant of European
decent living in a city on a different island. Within the national context of
Fiji, there are economic and political tensions accompanying its religious
diversity. Muslims in Fiji are a part of the East Indian settler community
which also includes many Hindu. Muslims are typically of a laboring class
on this agricultural island and are often renters and laborers in the sugar
cane fields. Indigenous Melanesian Fijians are a land-owning class whose
lifestyle may be associated closely with the land or they may derive income
from leasing their land. Politically, there have been tensions between the
Indigenous and the East Indian communities with regard to blue laws
protecting Sabbath observance on Sundays and with regard to the question of whether or not the Constitution should declare Fiji a Christian
nation. These questions had made it difficult to even establish a national
Constitution.

Possible meanings the speaker might bring

Now let us interpret the encounter in the case by starting at the top of the
grid. What are the possible meanings the speaker might be intending by
his question? The speaker, of course is an Indigenous Melanesian Christian
who is Methodist. While much of the sermon attended to statements about
Jesus, it is noticeable that this congregant's question does not refer to Jesus
explicitly. Therefore his question may simply indicate his interest in the
relationship between Christianity and Islam more generally—an interest
perhaps stimulated by the sermon and indicating a desire to discuss the

topic of interfaith relations further. Perhaps his interest is heightened by the Fijian social situation and the tensions between the different religious groups. He may be interested in the implications of interfaith dialog for the government. Or he may be curious about the relationship of both cultural groups to the land. The question may arise from a more personal level. The speaker might be considering converting to Islam, changing his own religion. (That is what the preacher originally suspects, according to the case.) Conversely, he might be interested in converting others to Christianity or perhaps engaging in more mutual interfaith dialog. He might even be suspicious of the preacher, testing the preacher's own commitments to Christianity. Short of suspicion, he may simply want to reinforce a sense of communion between them. An important element to his question might be the need to sense common identity and mutuality between guest and host, between preacher and congregant. The question might not be an inquiry into how "true" the religions are in any objective sense outside of actual community, and it might be the community itself that is of greater concern.[9]

Possible meanings the listener might bring

What are the possible meanings I the listener might hold? I may be more immediately puzzled in this encounter by the word "better" than by the multiple nuances attached to the word "religion." This is not my kind of question. The question of "better" to my mind might pertain to historical accuracy, to reliability concerning spiritual matters, or to the capacity of the religion to draw one closer to God. Since my sermon focused largely on the way Jesus is portrayed in the Qur'an, "better" might refer to a better Christology. Which religion describes Jesus most accurately, reliably or helpfully? At a personal level, as the preacher I would be wondering about the implications of this question for my preaching. Was I so muddy in my delivery that I left more questions than clarity? Conversely, was I so persuasive of the merits of Islam as to convince him to consider shifting his religious allegiance?

9. I have previously reflected on the relationship between truth and community in the Fijian context. See Bush, "Theological Education."

Possible similarities

What are the possible similarities between us as speaker and listener? While we have different cultural heritages, we have much in common. We have a common interest in religion, in religious expression, and in the meaningfulness of worship. We both seem to have an honest desire to serve God. We also share a desire for God to bless Fiji so that there would be flourishing among the people and on the land. Also, though we are talking together about the Qur'an, we are both Christians and Methodists. Among the possible respective interpretations listed above, two matters of interest or concern seem quite similar. The first is an interest in the very subject of a comparison between Christianity and Islam. The second is the matter of the relationship between the two of us. Different though we may be culturally, we may both want to affirm that we are participating in the same religious communion.

Possible differences

What are the possible differences between us? We have many cultural differences, not least of which is our respective first languages, which shape our thinking and communicating when we meet. On this particular subject of the relationship between Christianity and Islam, though, I suspect contextual factors play a major role in our respective consideration. The speaker lives closely to the local realities of the relation between the different religious communities in Fiji. This involves both ongoing cooperation in life together in Fiji and levels of estrangement from one another politically, culturally and economically. Also Fijian soldiers are frequently deployed in peace-keeping missions in the Middle East, so he might have more direct familiarity than I do with ongoing tensions between religious communities in the Middle East. While I too live in Fiji, my thinking about the relationship between Christianity and Islam might be shaped more by an understanding of European history and the Crusades as well as ongoing contemporary conflicts around the world. Though I am the preacher on this occasion, the question is admittedly more academic than immediate for me, and shaped by my reading on the subject.

Possible responses

My possible responses to his question include the following options. I can opt to answer his question by declaring one or the other religion as the "better" one. If I name Christianity as the better of the two, that might reassure him but also might reestablish a kind of cognitive equilibrium cutting short his thinking about the subject and our conversation together. I can try to explain myself further regarding my theology of the Trinity or my Christology or my understanding of the two religious traditions. Though I have already asked one clarifying question, I could turn the conversation further in his direction by asking him about his own thoughts, beliefs and commitments. I could shift topics of conversation toward tangents such as the need for national unity or interfaith relations. Finally, I could address the matter of common identity by affirming my own Methodist identity.

Most generous responses

Of these possible responses, which might be most generous to the speaker? Two in particular strike me as generous. To affirm our common identity as Methodists and to engage him in further conversation on the topic are both responses that take him and his question seriously and respectfully. Each has a slightly less generous downside. Affirming our common Methodist identity could be done in such as way as to undermine any growing inter-religious good will. Explaining my own thinking further honors his question but focuses more on me. Therefore, asking him further about his own beliefs seems to me the more respectful way to continue the conversation, so long as I don't dismiss his request for my further opinion. On the face of it, other options—such as shifting the topic or ending the conversation abruptly with a decisive answer—seem less generous.

The difficulty in choosing a generous response in this case lies in the immediate context and the temporary nature of this relationship. It is difficult in any conversation in a receiving line after worship to go into much detail on the subject. This is one of the frustrations of being a preacher. A good sermon does raise questions, but only some congregations provide a regular forum in which these questions can be further addressed. In Fiji, when a group of visitors are staying in a village, there is usually more time for fellowship and conversation during the visit, but not so in this case.

Conclusion

In conclusion, then, my initial choice would be to affirm our common Methodist identity but to do so in a way that keeps the conversation alive for subsequent attention. I would want to say something like, "Oh, I myself am a Methodist and I believe that we are a truthful religion, but I also have a lot of respect for Islam and I wish God's blessing for all Fiji's people—Christian, Muslim and Hindu." I would hope he would receive this response as a generous one in answer to his question, and I would hope, too, to have further opportunity to converse and to explore together during the course of the visit.

Sue Withers

Beginning with the authentic self

I reflect on our case mindful of who I am. I am a 54-year old Australian woman of French/English heritage who has lived her life in urban Melbourne. I attended an Anglican girl's college for my schooling, went to a Melbourne university, trained as a teacher and eventually moved into theological study and ministry within the Uniting Church. At first glance it can seem a straightforward narrative, without rough edges, but dig a bit deeper and my authentic self is far more frayed and complex. Add to the narrative the death of a mother at a young age, five children, a divorce, a remarriage, a new family, three step children, aging parents, and life takes on a more complex hue. Add to the narrative an ever-increasing awareness of my own frailty, uncertainty about the place of the Church in the 21st century and it is clear my readiness to approach any pastoral situation and theological reflection comes with a kaleidoscope of human experience and reference points.

My own faith journey has consequently had many inevitable twists and turns. I came to faith from a conservative evangelical theological position which claimed a clear, black and white understanding of the Bible, theology and place of the Christian disciple. Over the years this position has been challenged in an attempt to make sense of life theologically. It has been re-shaped and confronted by my own human frailty, sense of failure, success, joy, and disappointment.

This is the authentic self I need to name before I reflect on any pastoral situation. This is the self I bring to every ministry event. With respect to this case, I experienced an event earlier in my life that becomes my conversation partner with it.

Conversation partners

I lived in Fiji some years ago when I began my theological study at the Pacific Theological College. At that time I was part of a week-long village intensive similar to the field trip described in our case. I was pregnant, fresh to theological study and the only European woman in the group, so I was understandably pretty vulnerable entering an unfamiliar cultural context.

The dominating feelings were of self-consciousness, discomfort and **surprisingly. . .. *shame*. Where did shame come from?**

Where did it come from, given that I am normally brimming with confidence and swagger? When we are faced with an experience of the church and the gospel where we feel we don't fit in and don't have ready answers, we feel discomfort and uncertainty inside. I was intellectually aware of the diversity of faiths and cultures within Fiji, but I was unprepared for what was happening to me internally. I was self-conscious and unsure of how I should be in a space where I was guest and also where there were expectations about how men and women should be. The ranking of Christian leaders confronted me. It was my brothers, not sisters, who were given the privilege of preaching, speech making and decision making. This was an uncomfortable space for one who had embraced an inclusive God.

That same self-consciousness surfaced when discussing interfaith issues, where a lack of certainty can be viewed as lacking faith or intellectual weakness. Paver talks about experiences like these being "holy disruptions." When an experience is a holy disruption it runs counter to our expectations. I think of the apostle Paul, who speaks of the grace of God that comes through human weakness.

Attentive to self-deception

Self-deception has an impact on our authentic self and on our relationship with God. Tackling our own self-deception has the goal of overcoming pain, embarrassment, self-contradiction, and power. We need the safe sacred places to reveal our own selves and allow the gospel to address us.

To sit with the uncertainty is confronting.

The question was asked: "So which is better? Which religion is better? Which is right?"

How do I answer this? The temptation is to take hold of the situation and become the expert, sort it out, take control, present the self that is sure, clear, and confident, but in reality I just don't know how to answer that question. It is I who has the questions, not the answers.

Where is God when I am feeling disconnected and not at ease in an environment? Where is God when I feel overlooked or misunderstood? Where is God when I feel shame? Where is God when I am holding my brothers and sisters—from any religion or culture—as children of God?

How do I understand truth? How do I understand the truth of my brothers and sisters from other faiths?

I think Christians, particularly the 'old hands,' find it hard to live with uncertainty. If something does not make sense or does not match up with our present theological position we are very uncomfortable. We are inclined to roll the eyes, create straw men to knock down, or even shoot bible verses at twenty paces. We talk of peace, and the need for peace is vast, but if something gives our long held belief a shake we want it settled, now.

My challenge in this pastoral situation is to understand and struggle with the man's authentic question.

"Which is better?" he asks.

New Horizons

What is more important is what happens next. It is not the answer that is so important. It is not my clever dialogue and water-tight theological response. There is an invitation at this point in time to enter a new space not knowing where it will go. It is in being willing to take in all that is happening at that point in time. My self-consciousness, my authentic history, my tradition, my tendency to want to take control, my fear of looking a fool and just enter an uncharted moment where God may reveal God's self in an unexpected way. What strength it takes to do this.

A relationship may begin, and it is this preparedness to enter a space that may result in change. We can be transformed by the spirit of God. God's revelation is not 'out there'—theology happens as we each struggle authentically to articulate and live in an ongoing relationship with God, other people, culture, and the creation. Paver assures us that when we are open and vulnerable—even pregnant, uncertain, scared—and are willing to engage with those influences which come before us, we will be changed.

God's revelation in our case study takes place within a particular human experience—in a little village in Fiji—where we are the guest.

"Which is better?" he asks.

"Tell me your story," I answer. "Let's see where God leads us, my friend, as we talk together opening our authentic selves to each other. We will be received by God through each other and we will be transformed."

QUESTIONS FOR DISCUSSION

1. Both authors steer their reflections toward personal and interpersonal dimensions of the case. If you were interested in making more explicit some of the theological dimension present here, how might you go about reflecting on this case?

2. Can you imagine other pastoral situations in which the use of either Bush's practical hermeneutics grid or Paver's transcendental method might be a good method for reflection?

BIBLIOGRAPHY

Bevans, Stephen B. *Models of Contextual Theology*. Faith and Culture Series. Maryknoll, NY: Orbis, 1992.

Bush, Joseph E. "What Island Are You From? Celebrating the Journey in a Diverse Culture and Context." Presented at Australia-New Zealand Association of Theological Field Educators (ANZATFE) Biennial Conference, Sydney Australia, November 19, 2009.

————. "Theological Education as Reflective Practice in South Pacific Cultures." *The Pacific Journal of Theology* 2.39 (2008) 25–49. http://www.spats.org.fj/wp-content/uploads/2013/10/Issue39.pdf

Paver, John E. *Theological Reflection and Education for Ministry: The Search for Integration in Theology*. Aldershot, UK: Ashgate, 2006.

12

Lack of Grace at Grace Church

Barbara Blodgett and Christina Zaker

INTRODUCTION

Blodgett:

I HAVE CHOSEN TO use a technique from narrative therapy adapted for congregations. Narrative therapy invites clients to re-tell the stories of their lives. Most of us have constructed narratives that defend or explain the meaning of our lives, and our belief in the truth of these narratives is often deeply held, whether deservedly or not. Narratives can limit our own self-understandings, but we can learn to deconstruct them and tell different, more accurate, and more hopeful ones. The same is true for communities like congregations. A congregation learns to tell the story of its past in such a way as to frame its present. Unfortunately, many congregations tell stories of themselves that unhelpfully limit their possibilities for flourishing.[1]

One of the main tenets of narrative theory is that "the person is not the problem; the problem is the problem."[2] Applied to congregations, this means that the attempt to pin blame on anyone, even a central and influen-

---

1. See Golemon, *Finding Our Story.*

2. Lawrence Peers, "Expeditions into What is Possible: Narrative Leadership and Deep Change," in ibid., 52.

tial individual, is a false (though attractive) approach. Problems take on a life of their own, operating through the congregational system and relying on it to keep them alive. Therefore, one technique useful to exposing and defusing a problem is to 'externalize' it. Once externalized, the problem is deprived of its force and can no longer construct meaning.

For my theological reflection on a congregational conflict, I have adapted an exercise created by a narrative theorist.[3] In a playful and even humorous way, the story of the conflict gets re-narrated from the perspective of The Problem. The Problem boasts of its success and thereby reveals "the strategies, the techniques, the deceits, and the tricks that [it] has resorted to in its efforts to get the upper-hand."[4] The Problem identifies its allies, that is, the soft spots of temptation and weakness that lead to a demoralized and divided community. The Problem also admits who its enemies are: those sources of wisdom and courage that ultimately prevail and 'defeat' it.

I typically gravitate toward pedagogical techniques that create distance between cases and their authors (role-plays, non-verbal exercises, theater techniques, and so on). When a group of reflectors takes ownership of a case, the result is its de- and re-construction. Turning their cases over to the imaginative powers of a trusted group also often gives authors just the distance they need to see their situation in a new light.

Zaker:

In my work, I have been deeply influenced by parable scholarship. Barbara Reid, William Herzog, John Donahue, and others provide a way to explore scripture as an imperative part of theological reflection.[5] These scholars have pointed out a common flow to biblical parables. They often begin with the familiar, inviting hearers into a narrative that is recognizable and predictable. But then there is always a surprising shift. Something catches the hearers by surprise and flips their familiar world on its head. As Reid puts it, "Jesus' parables do not stay at the level of the familiar. Always there is a catch. . .they are startling and confusing, usually having an unexpected twist that leaves the hearers pondering what the story means and what it

3. White, "Externalising the Problem."

4. Ibid.

5. Reid, *Parables for Preachers*; Herzog, *Parables as Subversive Speech*; Donahue, *The Gospel in Parable*.

demands."[6] Parables end in an open-ended way with some new vision—usually pointing to God's nearness and preference for the marginalized—and hearers are invited to respond.

Drawing upon the notion that theological reflection carves out a similar type of reflective space as parables do, I have defined theological reflection this way: *"Theological reflection at its best is a communal effort to discern God's presence in the world, to carve the space for that presence to invite us into a new vision, and to lay the groundwork for that new vision to take root in how we live our lives."*[7] We are invited into the familiar narrative of a case, and through reflection and exploration we are invited to see it with new eyes.

Theological reflection in a parabolic mode flows through three steps that keep the discussion focused on discerning God's nearness. We begin by asking what is familiar about the narrative. What makes sense or is predictable about the way people acted or the way the narrative moved? In this first part we draw on the sources of scripture, tradition and context, asking what is similar between these sources and the narrative. We might ask why are things 'done this way' in our context or in our tradition. We might find a particular scripture that parallels and sheds light on the narrative.

Second, we ask what surprised us in the narrative. We look at what is uncomfortable or shocking. What challenged us because it turned our expectations upside down? What about the surprises in the narrative give insight into God's movement? (If nothing surprised us, we ask why, or what should have.) In the surprise, we are offered a glimpse of God's nearness in the narrative. The surprising moments offer us a chance to ask how this vision challenges us to respond with good news.

In the final step in theological reflection in parabolic mode we look at the narrative for ways we have seen God's movement in the actions or decisions of people in the narrative. We ask where there was good news in this experience and how we might cultivate it in our ministry. How might our actions become more surprising—more in line with the vision God offers? We conclude the reflection with an open ended stance.

---

6. Reid, *Parables for Preachers*, 7.

7. Zaker, "Parabolic Mode," 136.

THE CASE

Not long after she arrived at Grace Church, Pastor Jane discovered in the accounts a designated fund for choir loft expansion. Eventually she learned the history of this fund. The church had undergone a major renovation shortly before she had arrived, and the congregation had decided at the time not to make any changes to the choir loft because the expense was too high. But since remodeling the choir loft had been on the list of desired projects, some money had been set aside for the future. In the process of learning this history, she suggested to one of the choir members that if the choir were too large for the choir loft, they could always sit in the pews with their families and simply come forward to sing the anthem from the dais rather than the choir loft. His curt response was to say that "all churches in this region have choir lofts." Jane assumed that he spoke for many if not most of the choir, and decided that since there was already a fund established, she would not rock the boat any more when it came to where the choir sat and sang.

About a year later a bequest to the church included a sizeable gift to the fund. This gift provided the impetus for a renewed discussion about the choir loft expansion project. In church council, someone suggested that a committee be formed and that the music minister should chair it. Jane was dubious about having a staff person chair the committee but was not sure how to voice her concern. She met with the music minister, and he put together a list of people who should be invited to serve on the committee, including mostly choir members. Jane added a few names of non-choir members to balance the group.

One Sunday shortly thereafter, most of the committee got together after church and began a conversation. The group that met only represented the choir. The music minister quickly apologized—he had intended to catch non-choir members either right before or right after worship, but a few were not in worship and a few left before he could invite them. From then on, updates on the project were announced at weekly choir rehearsals, but no effort was made to reconvene the group who met the first time, nor was any effort made to include those who were originally on the list but had never actually been invited to serve.

Eventually Jane figured out that the "committee," which now was in effect the choir, was not sufficiently representative of other constituencies, who represented other ideas about the use of the fund. In fact there *were* other ideas circulating—she was hearing suggestions that instead of simply enlarging the choir loft, they might also expand the dais to better accommodate the Children's Christmas Play, occasional instrumental groups, and other possible liturgical activities. She relayed these ideas, and her concerns about representation, to the music minister, and they planned another committee meeting to address the project more broadly. Everyone on the original list was invited and with one exception, all attended. At the meeting Jane attempted to describe how the process had unfolded, that expanding the choir loft was a valuable idea, but that other proposals for use of the fund should be considered. As a result, a few of the choir members took offense, feeling that she was trying to manipulate the process. They quickly left the meeting in disgust. Without having to check, Jane knew there was a heated "parking lot meeting" after they adjourned.

A month later, however, she insisted that the committee meet again. Two proposals were put forth, and then someone suggested the idea of combining the two. Remarkably, the previously offended choir members voted for the combination project. Jane did not end up having to take a side regarding which proposal she supported, even though she had a preference. Today, the church has an expanded choir loft *and* an expanded dais.

REFLECTION

Barbara Blodgett

Hello. I am pleased to introduce myself: I am The Problem in this case, and my name is Suppressing Voices. Even before Pastor Jane arrived at Grace Church, I had been laying the groundwork for the conflict that erupted over the choir loft expansion. It did take me a while to succeed in getting people really angry at one another, but sometimes the seeds of conflict need to be sown gradually and quietly, so that no one notices them until it's too late. My particular specialty—the thing I do that makes me so good at being a Problem—is to exploit people's weaknesses and turn their virtues into vices. So let me tell you how it really went down.

One small accomplishment I scored early on was the naming of the fund itself. When plans for expanding the whole front area of the church were scuttled due to insufficient funds, I cleverly got folks to set aside some money in a fund that they agreed to call Choir Loft Expansion Fund rather than some more comprehensive name. That fooled people into thinking the money could be used for nothing else. They thought they were being helpfully precise, but instead, the name of the fund would later suppress their vision and discernment. Incidentally, Problems like me always have an ally in money, because there's never enough of it. Scarcity aggrieves people, makes them all the more anxious and cautious about the resources they *do* have, and causes them to lose the good sense and wisdom they normally bring to decision-making. As one of my enemies, the astute Presbyterian pastor John W. Wimberly, Jr. once wrote, "Money is money. Either a congregation has it or it doesn't. When a congregation has very limited financial resources to apply to facilities, wise and effective management becomes even more important."[8] I am proud to say that with the help of my friend Scarcity, I succeeded in making management at Grace Church less wise and less effective.

But I digress. When Pastor Jane stumbled across the fund and started asking around about it, I got momentarily worried. She likes to include all perspectives and ideas, and I knew she might try to get people actually talking to one another and thereby avert conflict. But I realized that I could capitalize on her aversion to conflict itself, a weakness she shares with many ordained ministers. I worked my magic on the choir member and helped him dismiss her inquiry with that ridiculous rejoinder that "all churches in this region have choir lofts." In her naiveté and desire to avoid getting entangled in managing the issue, she quieted down. Score one more for me!

Then the gift of new funding came in. A few more people, some of whom wanted a bigger choir loft and others who wanted a bigger dais, remembered that at one time the plans were never quite settled. In true Protestant fashion, one of them suggested forming a committee. I was concerned that it might become a well-functioning deliberative group, so I got immediately to work and made sure that the music minister was appointed chair. One of the best ways to suppress voices is to put someone in charge of decision making who has a great deal of self-interest invested in one particular outcome. He would be inclined to make sure the vote went in his direction. I was also able to exploit the extent to which congregations like this one are enamored with democratic process and not very good at the practice of discernment. As congregational consultant Dan Hotchkiss has written, congregations "absorb the organizational forms they see around them" in the culture, including that "laity speak their most authoritative word by voting."[9] I knew any decision favored by the majority would appear

8. Wimberly, Jr., *Business of the Church,* 73.

9. Hotchkiss, *Governance and Ministry,* 35.

'fair' to this congregation. Finally, I could rely on Jane. Despite sensing that something was wrong with letting a staff person chair the committee—someone with authority by virtue of role who could not help but exercise undue influence—she again chose silence over leadership. She might at this point have helped her congregation understand good governance principles and teach them some skills of prayerful discernment, but I prevented her from recognizing the opportunity. Her oversight allowed the conflict to continue to fester quietly.

I caused the music minister conveniently to 'forget' to contact all the committee members ahead of time for the after-church meeting. He fell back on his well-honed habit of failing to plan sufficiently for meetings. He made the excuse of having assumed an informal and personal approach would suffice—catching people before and after worship. And people readily forgave him. After all, people so love to believe that smaller churches are just like families, and that their members can dispense with impersonal formalities like contacting each other during the week, because "everybody'll be at church." They fondly quote Bible passages like Ephesians 2:19 where Paul refers to the church as "the household of God," forgetting that even households need effective communication, and also forgetting that Paul wasn't really talking about choir loft expansion meetings in the first place. If anything, his favored image of the body of Christ emphasizes the need to respect even those members of the community who might go ignored.

So, conversations about expanding the choir loft went along, and the music minister continued simply to bring updates to the choir at its rehearsals instead of actually going to the effort of calling another meeting. The choir came to think of itself as the committee and became all the more invested in their ideas for expanding the choir loft. My campaign of suppressing voices was going really well.

And then Pastor Jane had the audacity to meet with the music minister and remind him that other renovation ideas were circulating among church members, ideas that deserved a hearing and consideration. She carefully planned a meeting where all voices would be heard, and I started to become nervous that I would never live to see the day when tempers would flare and feelings would be hurt. But I was vindicated. I fanned the flame under the choir members' sense of entitlement to be the ones influencing worship-related decisions in the church. I encouraged them to interpret Jane's leadership as "manipulation." It's a classic move to blame the leader when she is attempting to change the way things are always done. Those annoyingly insightful leadership theorists that so many pastors have read over the years, Ron Heifetz and Marty Linsky, write about good leaders who "hold steady in the heat of action," the way Jane was learning to do, and prevent becoming the issue themselves.[10] I did briefly manage to get Jane doubting herself in a brilliant move where she "collude[d] unwittingly with [her] marginalizers."[11] She wondered whether she *was*, in fact, manipulating the situation by appearing to defend one side over the other when she was only trying to surface all ideas. I cheered with glee as committee members stomped out of the meeting. My campaign of division and suppression reached its height in my all-time favorite expression: the Parking Lot Meeting, where people let loose talking behind each other's backs.

In the end, though, I am chagrined to report that as The Problem I failed to keep things a mess. Eventually the people at Grace Church listened to one another, sought compromise on a few details, and came up with a renovation plan that everybody could live with. I made one last-ditch effort with Pastor Jane. Because of me, she ignored her own blossoming leadership instincts and succumbed to a confusion I enjoy perpetuating within ministers. She thought that she should remain silent regarding the renovation proposals out of a belief that neutrality is 'pastoral.' She momentarily weakened in her role as a leader mobilizing people to seek a future of new and creative possibilities. But, in the end, I regret to conclude that despite my best efforts, Grace Church worked it out and has ultimately been strengthened in its worship and witness to the glory of God.

Christina Zaker

Recognizing the Familiar

There is so much that resonates as familiar in this case. As with almost any conflict narrative, there are bruised egos, one-sided discussions, selective memory, failure in follow-through, stacked committees, manipulative behavior, turf battles, and conflicts of interest. These are the tropes of church conflict, and they make church leaders weary. This particular narrative also contains problems that reflectors quickly recognize: money dictating process rather than communal needs, the lack of a coherent congregational mission that could inform the decision, and leaders needing to be the ones

10. Heifetz and Linsky, *Leadership on the Line*, 141.

11. Ibid., 35.

who insist on diverse representation in decision-making. At the same time, there are also familiar elements to celebrate in this case: generous people leaving bequests to the church, and leaders both lay and ordained who care enough about quality worship to argue over how to invest time and money in it.

What scripture passages add to our reflection on these familiar elements in the story? If one of the central challenges identified in this narrative is how Pastor Jane might encourage her staff to be open to different opinions, then Matthew 5:46 ("For if you love those who love you, what reward do you have? Do not even the tax collectors do the same?") is relevant. This passage challenges Jane. When a battle is brewing, church members are like the tax collectors and pagans. They almost instinctively seek out their friends rather than their enemies in order to shore up their side. Jane will have to remember that openness to different opinions is never as easy as it sounds; it is akin to loving one's enemies! Matthew 6:33 also comes to mind because of the way it tells hearers not to worry, but to seek first the Kingdom. It provides nuance to Jane's own hesitation to speak or direct the process at the beginning of the narrative. Might her lack of leadership at the beginning be rooted more in worry rather than in wanting to "seek first the Kingdom"? Finally, with regard to scripture, Matthew 21:33–41 (the Parable of the Landowner and the Tenants) also speaks to this case. This parable might suggest that when pastors do all the work of cultivating "the field" and preparing it for collaborative leadership, it can't be then simply left to its own; there is still room for mentoring and guidance.

There are familiar themes when we engage theological and contextual voices as well. Communities often struggle to determine who has a say in the use and structure of liturgical space. There are factions that would point to the pastor; others would point to the choir or minister of music; still others would argue that the whole community should have a voice in the discussion. The common priesthood of all the baptized seems to have played a role in Pastor Jane's evolving insistence that the committee have adequate representation. Another theme that is common in ministry is the role of silence. Pastor Jane's silence at the beginning seemed to come from a stance of fear, but her silence in the final meeting seems to come from a stance of empowering others and allowing the Spirit to guide the process. Scriptures such as Mark 13:11 ("do not worry beforehand about what you are to say; but say whatever is given you at that time") or Ezekiel 3:1 (when Ezekiel is encouraged to eat the scroll) challenge reflectors to trust that if they are focused on bringing God's word into the discernment process, then the Spirit will give them the words to say.

Seeking the Surprise

Theological reflection in a parabolic mode encourages reflectors to look at the narrative a second time with an eye for what is surprising. One surprise reflectors might note is that regardless of the conflict that took place, the Spirit is still evident in the decision. Somehow it did not matter that there was an initially tentative leader, evasive staff, and divisive community members. In the end, with persistent encouragement, they did come together to discern an appropriate response. Matthew 18:20 ("For where two or more are gathered in my name, I am there among them") suggests that the effort it takes to bring people together and to allow all voices to be heard is time well spent because it is in community that the Spirit bears fruit.

A second surprise is the evolution of Pastor Jane's understanding of herself as a leader. She seemed to start out with tentative questions, remaining silent out of worry, then began making suggestions, and finally "insisted" that the group come together again to discern. In the end, she did not need to say what she thought should happen, but could allow the community to discern a response. This evolution was a reminder that *metanoia* happens as leaders grow more authentic to their call.

Acknowledging the Invitation

Each of these moments of surprise offered an invitation to see with new eyes how this narrative is Good News. One invitation is to trust the Spirit. Despite our flawed process and individual egos, the Spirit still invites us to collaborate in the mission to build the Kingdom of God. It is important for ministers to realize that although we are not perfect in ministry, if we seek first the Kingdom, then God will help our efforts bear fruit. This insight gives reflectors several different invitations: the invitation to accept that our imperfect selves can be used in God's plan, the reminder to "seek first the Kingdom" in the process of ministerial decisions, and encouragement to be persistent in fostering collaborative discernment.

Pastor Jane's evolution as a leader also touched on the invitation to trust. Reflectors are invited to see her evolving leadership as encouragement for our own journey as leaders. The image of Ezekiel consuming the scroll suggests that trust in the Spirit stems from our ability to be grounded in the word of God. The invitation might be to be intentional about the ways leaders encourage their community to be so grounded. Better articulation and awareness of congregational mission statements, more intentional invitations to prayer and discernment, and seeking the voices of those without power in times of discernment are all ways leaders might invite the Spirit to guide their work.

The invitations to be more confident in our evolving leadership, trusting the Spirit's guidance and grounded in the word of God are Good News! Grace is abundant at Grace Church—we only need eyes that can see.

QUESTION FOR DISCUSSION

1. Have you found ways to do theological reflection by turning the familiar and ordinary into the surprising and dramatic?

BIBLIOGRAPHY

Donahue, John R. *The Gospel in Parable: Metaphor, Narrative and Theology in the Synoptic Gospels*. Philadelphia: Fortress, 1998.

Golemon, Larry A., ed. *Finding Our Story: Narrative Leadership and Congregational Change*. Narrative Leadership Collection. Herndon, VA: Alban Institute, 2010.

Heifetz, Ronald A., and Marty Linsky. *Leadership on the Line: Staying Alive through the Dangers of Leading*. Boston: Harvard Business School Press, 2002.

Herzog, William R. *Parables as Subversive Speech: Jesus as Pedagogue of the Oppressed*. Louisville: Westminster John Knox, 1994.

Hotchkiss, Dan. *Governance and Ministry: Rethinking Board Leadership*. Herndon, VA: Alban Institute, 2009.

Reid, Barbara E., OP. *Parables for Preachers: Year B, The Gospel of Mark*. Collegeville, MN: Liturgical, 1999.

White, Michael. "Externalising the Problem." *Michael White Workshop Notes*. Published September 21, 2005. www.dulwichcentre.com.au

Wimberly, Jr., John W. *The Business of the Church: The Uncomfortable Truth that Faithful Ministry Requires Effective Management*. Herndon, VA: Alban Institute, 2010.

Zaker, Christina. "Theological Reflection in Parabolic Mode." DMin diss. Catholic Theological Union, 2012.